RIDING THE BEHEMOTH

Spiritual, Nutritional Information and Financial
Advice for Canadian Patients and Their
Families Who Face Breast Cancer

ARL T. CORNELL

iUniverse, Inc.
Bloomington

RIDING THE BEHEMOTH
Spiritual, Nutritional Information and Financial Advice for Canadian
Patients and Their Families Who Face Breast Cancer

iUniverse books may be ordered through booksellers or by contacting:

iUniverse
1663 Liberty Drive
Bloomington, IN 47403
www.iuniverse.com
1-800-Authors (1-800-288-4677)

ISBN: 978-1-4759-8364-7 (sc)
ISBN: 978-1-4759-8365-4 (e)

Library of Congress Control Number: 2013905870

Printed in the United States of America

iUniverse rev. date: 5/29/2013

Cover design by Joela Maglalang

CONTENTS

ACKNOWLEDGEMENTS

After we were born we were loved, taken care of, guided through maturity and helped to understand the meaning of life. Along with our life, there are always challenges and obstacles to face and to learn to fight, manage and accept, whatever the end result. We find strength in what remains behind, and we become better people.

I would like to thank my husband, Ferdinand, for continuous support; my daughters Gianne, 13, and Krizia Mae, 10, who did a great job to make our house a home; and my wonderful boy, JR, 8, who called himself the maintenance guy of the house.

To my mother-in-law, Victoria, and my mom, Crispina, who are always around me and are very caring and supportive.

And to my friends Lorna Cooper-Roxas, Emy Corpuz and Gloria Duro, and my cousins Josie Gonzalez and Ate Lily. To my friends and relatives around the globe who touch my life: thank you for all the spiritual support!

INTRODUCTION

I was imbued with spirit to write this book, which will serve as an additional resource to people who are diagnosed with illness, anyone who is about to undergo treatment or anybody who is touched by someone who is suffering.

I was at a loss when I was diagnosed with breast cancer. I did not know what to do next, and I did not know exactly what to expect. Many patients who are undergoing their first cycle of treatment have many questions in their minds that they cannot get the answer to right away. One time while I was waiting for my turn in the waiting area, I met some patients who were on their second and third cycle, and I was anxious to ask what they had gone through so that I would know what to expect, even though I might not experience things the same way they had. As explained by the nurse during my orientation, every individual has a different experience.

Now that I have experienced all of this, I know exactly how it feels to ride the Behemoth. The behemoth and the Behemoth ride are the best metaphors that I can create for the word "cancer." It was in 2010 when my kids rode on the Behemoth, a roller coaster in

Canada's Wonderland. It is so huge and runs at high speed with twists and turns and double-back flat loops and horizontal loops, as well as eight extreme drops. Everyone who rode on it couldn't believe they survived the whirls, twists and drops. My kids described the ride as "so sick." Yes, that was their word, which they meant as scary, breathtaking and insane. This was exactly what I felt while undergoing my treatment. Everyone has a different experience, but I will describe mine as the Behemoth ride.

In the Bible, Job questions God because he suffers disastrous experiences. God refers to the behemoth in Job 40:15. The behemoth is a biblical creature that cannot be identified. It is a kind of monster that has so much strength and enormous power that no one can beat or control it. The behemoth exists because God created it, and only he can destroy it. Thus I often ask God, "Why me? Am I not a good citizen? Is this a kind of a test?" But it is useless to question God regarding why I suffered such an illness. Our life is borrowed from him, and it is only he who can take our lives back; we just don't know when.

Cancer is an illness that can strike anyone; it will choose any age, gender, race or profession at any time. The illness has taken our loved ones, people we know, their children and their children's children. Cancer is strong like a beast, but humans are also relentless; we just need to learn how to ride and fight.

When I was diagnosed with stage III breast cancer in February 2010, I felt horrible and was in pain, and it seemed to be unjust. I cried a river and had many questions in my mind. My family has no history of breast cancer; I am an average person who has a simple life. As I am passing through it, day by day I am getting answers. God is giving me more time to stay because maybe he wanted me to be closer to him. I was born Catholic and I go to church, but to tell you the truth, I seldom pray. I don't know how to say the rosary, but I thought as long as I didn't do bad things and was fair to all, then I did not need to pray. I was quite embarrassed when I told my friend Thelma that I did not know how to pray the rosary, so she taught me.

I thought about ways to serve God. I told my family to be active in our parish church, to do altar serving, to be ushers and to be members of the choir. I learned how to be more forgiving, be more loving and find time to serve my community to the best that I could. My husband, mother and I are attending charity events to support our church. I would like to support Sunny Brook Hospital, Scarborough Hospital and Hearth Place, a cancer support centre in order to fulfil my goal, should I get well.

I spend my time in the library to look for books to enhance my medical and nutritional knowledge, and I visit reliable websites for easy access of information. My healthcare team, especially my oncologist, explained how he staged my cancer and what treatment was appropriate to my situation. Truthfully, I do not understand most of the medical terminologies, but the book he gave me, which was written by a group of oncologists and was created by Amgen Canada, helped me to understand and educated me about my therapy and staging my cancer.

Before my chemotherapy treatment, a nurse oriented me about the treatment and gave me a head start about food and nutrition to be eaten after each cycle of treatment that would give me strength and energy, and food to be eaten once nausea and vomiting occurred. She gave me pamphlets, brochures and more information that the Canada Cancer Society has supplied and written for reference. I am a diabetic and have high blood pressure, so I was also recommended to meet with my dietician. I have to attend a nutritional class in the diabetic clinic. This was the first time that I'd heard about "My Plate" regarding the daily intake of a balanced diet and "always go with the rainbow" regarding fruits and vegetables.

As soon as my friends, colleagues and relatives knew about my illness, they continuously gave me information regarding what to eat that could cure cancer. It was so overwhelming that I didn't know how reliable the information was, so that prompted me to research food that could fight cancer. There were lots of fruits and vegetables to choose from, but I have chosen the most popular ones that I could easily buy and that had the best fighting nutrients.

Before my mastectomy, I had to meet with my plastic surgeon for possible reconstruction on the same day. She explained my options and the reconstruction procedure if I qualified to be a candidate. It was a scary thought for me because I had not heard of anyone that I knew who had experienced such an operation, but I was interested. This concept urged me to scrutinize the procedure, so I did more research on websites and read the Canada Cancer Society information booklet that my plastic surgeon gave me.

I read that two factors that could possibly contribute to getting breast cancer are one's lifestyle and one's eating habits. I was so curious how lifestyle and eating habits could really be the factors, so I read anything about those topics in magazines, newspapers and on websites.

Many people are financially devastated by a disease such as cancer, and I want to give information and educate people as to what to do once an illness strikes. As a financial advisor for 17 years and a mortgage broker for 5 years, I believe that I have a social obligation and fiduciary responsibility to relay my experience and expertise in this field to all walks of life.

THE BEHEMOTH RIDE

The Start

Early one morning, I woke up in my nightgown with a dried, splattered brown colour on my left chest. I ignored it because I thought it was just the drool from my young boy, who slept beside me that night. It took several days before I saw another dime-size spot of dried blood on my bra. This was when I thought of consulting my family doctor, in October 2009. My doctor asked me to have a mammogram. Mind you, after my very first mammogram, which I'd experienced in 2008, I swore not to have any mammogram tests anymore, because I really felt the pain when the two parts squeezed my breasts. But I figured I needed to do it again.

The clinic that I was referred to had given me its earliest open appointment, which was in March 2010. I went back to my doctor, and she gave me a list of clinics that could examine me the soonest. I found a clinic that was 60 kilometres away from my home that could perform the test on December 23, 2009.

On that day in the waiting room, a mature lady came

out and called my name, and I found her very calm and trustworthy. She was so gentle in assisting me throughout the examination, and I did not feel any pain compared to what I'd felt before—but I was weakened by the blood that splattered on the machine as soon as the two panels of the machine squeezed my left breast. I was shivering with nervousness while the technician lost her composure. My thoughts were dark, and I wanted some answers to what was on my mind in that moment. There was a note in front of the machine saying, "The technician cannot discuss anything with you; please talk to your doctor." I still asked the technician about what were the possibilities of blood discharge on the nipple. She answered quietly that it could be an infection or something else. She directed me to the ultrasound section for further examination.

Agony

The day of my breast examination changed my life—I felt I was not the same person. I knew there was something about my health, but I didn't know how severe it was. I can't stress how much I cried and wondered every sleepless night, but I kept silent. I never told anyone, not even my husband or mother, because I didn't want them to worry. Besides, Christmas was coming, and everyone should be merry for the holiday. I managed to hide my emotions and feelings, but this was really painful and difficult for me because I had no idea what the prognosis would be. I was not yet thinking clearly, but I did pretend and did what I normally did.

My family doctor was set to see me in January 2010, and she referred me to a doctor who had lots of experience with breasts. I went to see this specialist at once, and the doctor scheduled me for more tests, including a biopsy. Meeting with all the staff and doctors that looked after me at the Scarborough General Hospital was definitely a pleasant experience; they were so gentle, calm and helpful. They have a lot of patience in dealing with such emotional patients like me.

In February 2010, I had to get the result of my tests. I had second thoughts about bringing my spouse with me, but it was a good thing that I brought him to listen to the results. I shed my tears as soon as I heard my doctor tell me, "You have a cancer." I didn't process the words she told me after that; she just explained and instructed my husband. She then scheduled me for a mastectomy on March 31, 2010.

Denial

I tried to assess myself. I stood at the mirror and looked at myself, and I murmured that there was nothing wrong with me. I felt so healthy; I was strong and had lots of energy. I couldn't believe that it was happening to me. I thought of a second opinion before having a mastectomy. I entertained people who talked about nonsurgical treatment and herbal medicine. I went to my family doctor, and she told me that I could consult different doctors for a second opinion. As she pulled out my record, it was indicated there that my case had been brought out by chance in a doctors' Multidisciplinary Case Conference, and they recommended the necessary treatment, which everyone agreed was a mastectomy. Having heard that, I changed my mind and did not consult another doctor, because that would confuse me more. I did lots of research regarding mastectomies and reconstruction, and I thought it was the best thing to do. I had my mind set to perform the mastectomy and immediate reconstruction.

THE FEAR

My Feelings

I always empathized with my clients who had cancer, enlightened some who survived, extended help and prayers to those who were still battling and sympathized with the families who were defeated. But now it was me that cancer had stricken, and it was totally different. At the moment of diagnosis, the way I thought had been changed. I felt different in many ways.

I had never experienced being admitted to the hospital, and I'd never had a surgery, so at this time I was worried that I might not wake up when they performed the mastectomy. I was thinking about my other health issues, which were high blood pressure and diabetes.

I had so many mix emotions: I was afraid, depressed and sad, and I felt helpless. I did not want to talk to anyone, because coping with this kind of illness was very stressful. What I wanted was to get rid of the cancer and to live longer.

My godmother, Amee, and godfather, Vic Andino, gave me a prayer for healing that comforted me. It was very sympathetic and meaningful as I read it over and over, and my tears dropped unnoticed each time. I would like to share it with you.

Lord, look upon me with eyes of mercy. May your healing spirit rest upon me. It is through your power that I was created. Since you created me from nothing, you can certainly recreate me. Fill me with the healing power of your spirit. May your life-giving powers flow into every cell of my body and into the depths of my soul. Mend what is broken. Cast out anything that should not be within me. Rebuild my brokenness.

Restore my strength for service in your kingdom. Touch my soul with your compassion for others. Touch my heart with your courage and infinite love for all. Touch my mind with your wisdom, that my mouth may always proclaim your praise. Teach me to reach out to you in my need, and help me to lead others to you by my example. Most loving heart of Jesus, bring me health in body and spirit so that I may serve you with all my strength.

My Kids

Every time I saw my kids, I cried. I was here for them, but I was questioning what their future would be, just in case. I didn't know how to relay to them, but I had to try. My eldest, who was 12 years old at that time, sensed that there was something wrong, so I revealed my illness to her and assured her that I would get well. I did talk to my younger kids, who were 9 years old and 6 years old, in simple ways, and I felt they understood.

I held back my tears when my youngest asked me, "Will you be here on my next birthday?"

I said, "Of course. Mommy will get well, and you have to pray for me." I told them what to expect when I went on my treatment, and I said their daily life might change because they'd have to help Dad as well. Although my eldest already knew how to do the laundry and cook rice, I trained them to clean the toilet and do more household work. My youngest volunteered to be the maintenance man of the house, and what he meant was to check for the lights and TV to be off when not in use. From then on, my kids were more loving, and my eldest never answered back if I asked her to do something. When my son misbehaved, his older sisters reprimanded him.

My Spouse
I asked my husband, "What now?" He bluntly said, "I will always be here." He also felt stressed. I often asked him many things, and I had always been honest about what I felt. Sometimes I avoided talking about my illness, which I thought it would ease both of our emotions. He was my number-one help in my situation, so I wanted him to know what I needed.

Business and Finances
My husband and I were both in financial business, and we managed a small insurance agency. I played a very important role in the company, and the most essential duty that I did was bookkeeping and managing the financial aspect of the business, which should be done on a daily basis. The challenging part was that no one could do the job; not even my husband would do it. I had pending transactions that should only be followed

up by me. There were a lot of personal, small things that should be addressed immediately, like errors on bills statement, that should be tackled within 30 days. There were disputes on major issues like taxes and installations that were already done. When it rained, it poured, and that was what happened while I was supposedly resting. Things were not favourable by then, but I learned how to ignore things for a period of time.

I told myself I couldn't be sick, but I was. I had time to do what I needed to do, one step at a time. First and foremost, my husband and I met with a lawyer to update our last will and testament. We prepared a different power of attorney. I sat down with my husband and checked everything we owned to help out our finances. We did review our life insurance, investments and the registered educational plan of our children, to see if all of them had a waiver of premium of disability. The sad thing to say was I did not have a critical illness plan because I was already suffering from high blood pressure and diabetes. You could apply for a regular critical illness insurance plan if you were healthy or there was another simplified application that could cover some illnesses, but I failed to qualify. The good thing was I had a short-term and long-term disability insurance that replaced my income and helped my family financially.

The Slope

I had never undergone any kind of surgery, so it was a kind of strange feeling to be in the hospital wearing a nightgown together with a bunch of people, waiting to be operated on. I wandered around and I felt like I was watching a movie. My nervousness still shivered my bones, and I tried to calm myself via TV. When I was on the stretch bed, they asked me to take off my eyeglasses as well, so I felt even more different because everything around me was blurry while my stretch bed rolled toward the operating room. When we were approaching the operating room, a young man said, "Aunt Arlyne, how are you?" I was so shocked that I thought I was in a different world. The young man, Jason Hombrebueno, was my nephew, and I had not seen him for ages. He worked as a nurse in the hospital, and he told me that he saw my name a week earlier on the surgery list. I was quite relieved to know someone had looked after me.

When I woke up after several hours, the first thing I touched was my left breast and then my tummy. I was so dismayed when I realized I was not reconstructed but my tummy was cut. I knew something went wrong, and I wanted to ask any doctor at that time, but to no avail. I felt so alone and in anguish. I was calmed down when Jason came to me with food that I needed to take at that time. I was lucky enough that I had someone with me all the time, and that comforted me. At last the two surgeons came to see me and explained to me that I had more lymph nodes that were positive of cancer, and that was why my plastic surgeon failed to continue. My plastic surgeon recommended I undergo treatment, which was chemotherapy and radiation, before reconstruction was done; they also wanted to fix my hernia.

I had the option to stay in the hospital for three days, but I chose to recover at home because I wanted to be with my family. I was so thankful that Canada had such wonderful health-care benefits. An alternate care setting (ACS) serving Durham Region, a subsidiary division of the Ontario Health Insurance Plan, provided nursing services seven days a week, including holidays. A nurse came to visit me seven days a week until my drain was clear and once every three weeks thereafter. It was up to me when I wanted them to look after me.

Meeting with My Team

After recovery from my surgery, I met with my team again. My team members were a surgeon who performed my biopsies (where he got cells or tissues removed from my body for examination to help with diagnosis), a surgical oncologist who was my surgeon (with specific training in treating cancer by removing lumps or tumours from my body), a pathologist (to look at the tissue from biopsies under a microscope to see if it has cancer cells), a medical oncologist (who specialized in the treatment of my cancer using different medications such as chemotherapy and drugs), a radiation oncologist (who specialized in the treatment of my cancer using radiation; he developed my treatment plan) and lastly a social worker who comforted me and my family regarding how to cope with cancer and its treatment. All the doctors, nurses, social workers and staff from Scarborough General Hospital and Sunny Brook Hospital, and the secretaries and receptionists of my doctors, were so caring, delicate and sweet—and not just one day but during the whole treatment I had. They were a group of people with a high education and with perfect character. Definitely I missed them, but I wished I wouldn't be seeing them for treatment.

Staging My Breast Cancer

As I said earlier, my medical oncology doctor explained to me how he staged my breast cancer. It was important to me to know what stage of cancer I had. I was nervous because I worried he'd say it was already terminal, and I would have been devastated by that.

Staging describes or classifies cancer according to the extent of cancer involvement within my body. I have learned that stage is determined by the size of the tumour mass, how much the tumour has spread to nearby tissues, whether or not the cancer has spread to the lymph nodes under the arm (axilla) and whether or not the cancer has spread to different parts of the body (liver, brain, bones or lungs).

When I was diagnosed with cancer, and when my oncologist had all the information he needed from other specialists, then that was the only time for him to stage and grade my cancer. The stage of a breast cancer describes the tumour size and tells whether it has spread beyond the place where it started to grow. In the earliest stage of breast cancer, cancer cells are found only in the milk ducts or lobules; this is called in situ cancer. If in situ cancer is diagnosed before the cells have spread to the surrounding tissue, there is no risk of them spreading after they have been removed.

When breast cancer spreads out of the duct or lobule, it is called invasive cancer. It can still be treated effectively if diagnosed early.

In my case I was staged to three: my cancer cells had spread to the lymph nodes and may have spread to nearby tissues, such as muscle or skin.

There are five stages in breast cancer. Stage zero has two kinds: Ductal carcinoma in situ (DCIS) are abnormal cells in the lining of a milk duct that have not spread outside the duct. The other kind is lobular carcinoma in situ (LCIS), which are abnormal cells in the lining of a lobule. Stage one is when the tumour is two centimetres or smaller, and the cancer has not spread outside the breast. Stage three is when the tumour is two to five centimetres, or the cancer has spread to the lymph nodes, or both. Stage four is when the cancer has spread to distant parts of the body.

There are also three grades of cancer cells. Grade one is low grade; bad cells are slow growing and less likely to spread. Grade two is moderate, and grade three is a high grade where the cells are aggressive and grow quickly (and they're more likely to spread).

Treatment
My plan was based on the stage of my disease, prognostic and predictive factors and my personal choices; my age and my premenopausal condition were also considered. Treatment used in administering breast cancer can be done in two different ways: local therapies (which treat the area of the tumour) and systemic therapies (which treat the entire body). Local treatments include surgery to remove the tumour or lump, and radiation to dissolve any cancer cells remaining at the site of the tumour. I had surgical removal first, which is normally performed, but if the tumour is large, then surgical removal is not necessary. The other way of treatment could be done by chemotherapy or hormonal therapy before surgery, which is common for some groups of women in many hospitals and which continues to be studied in clinical trials for a variety of reasons.

Some women prefer to have the chemotherapy and radiation before surgery, to save their breast. I was lucky enough that my surgeon had opened up my case during their scheduled conference meeting, and the group of doctors recommended the mastectomy. I had the mastectomy first, and during the procedure they found more lymph nodes that were positive and removed them. Chemotherapy and radiation treatment followed. I thought that if I'd had the chemotherapy and radiation performed first, my lymph nodes that were positive might not have found, because they were not visible via biopsy tests and the mammogram.

Chemotherapy and radiation were systemic therapies that should be done to demolish my tumour cell growth and to eliminate any tumour that behaved abnormally. Another therapy that I had to undergo was to take hormonal drug therapy for five years. My oncologist told me that this would help me to be well; he said that it was the most systematic way to slow the growth and prevent my cancer cells from spreading.

It is good to know what kind of receptor you have so that your doctor or nurses can discuss the treatment options for you. A receptor is like a lock on the outside of a cell that is only opened by the right substance. When the receptor is opened, it causes a specific event to occur, which is part of the body's normal function. HER2 is a type of receptor that is opened by growth factor, and it makes cells grow. I have more HER2 receptors than normal, so I have cancer cells that are called HER2-positive, which grows more quickly than other types of cancer. The other receptor, called HER2-negative, means one has more normal HER2 receptors.

Women have sex hormones, which is the estrogen produced in the body, and doctors aim to reduce or block the action of estrogen on the hormone receptor by giving hormonal therapy. The therapy prevents the hormones from stimulating tumour growth and helps to destroy tumour cell. The drug that I would be taking was Tamoxifen. This drug has been used for a while and is a renowned hormonal therapy for receptor-positive premenopausal and postmenopausal women with breast cancer. This drug produces multiple hormonal actions, but it stimulates an estrogen-like effect on the lining of the uterus, the cardiovascular system and the bones.

Chemotherapy was used for my treatment. Some wrong notions about chemo are that having side effects means that the drugs are working, and not having side effects means the drugs are not working. Side effects are different to every individual, and everyone has different drugs to be taken—but side effects don't correspond to the treatment working or not working. Chemotherapy has been shown to help rates of survival for those younger than the age of 50, and it reduces rates of relapse. Chemotherapy is more often administered as a combination of drugs, called a regimen. Chemotherapy drugs slow or even stop the cancer cells from growing, multiplying or spreading to other parts of my body. Different chemotherapy drugs destroy cancer cells in different ways. A combination of drugs eliminate more tumour cells than a single drug, leading to a higher chance of cure. For me, there were six chemotherapy cycles for four months; a cycle length was three weeks. I took a regimen of Fluorouracil, Epirubicin, Cyclophosphanmide (into vein) and AKA FEC for the first three cycles, followed by docetaxel for three cycles.

Radiation was necessary as a part of my treatment. Radiotherapy uses a special beam of radiation therapy, by using ionizing radiation. This was complementary to my chemotherapy treatment. Said radiation targets the affected area and tries to eliminate any bad cells remaining. The doses of radiation are called fractions. I had been given one fraction daily, done Monday through Friday. Cancer cells divide rapidly, and they are more likely to be affected by repeated, daily doses. Over the course of radiation treatment, the number of tumour cells steadily declines until hopefully all the cancer cells are killed. Normal cells can recover after each radiation dose, in about three to six hours. Normal cells could be damaged as well, even after many weeks of treatment have passed, but they will recover in due time. Radiation will not be used if the cancer reoccurs in the same area.

The Bow

Orientation

An oncology nurse educated me on a lot of things in half a day. She talked about all the drugs that would be administered to me, their side effects and what to do in every cycle. This was overwhelming to me, but it seemed like I was on a raft that ran through the flow until an anchor stopped the raft. I couldn't stop being emotional. As I walked down the corridor toward the clinic, there were people waiting for their turn to enter the clinic. Upon seeing the clinic, I was amused because I thought I would be lying down on bed alone in a room—but what I saw was like a huge beauty parlour with approximately 15 chairs, which were all occupied by cancer patients who had different cases, ages and genders. They seemed so happy, and they were talking, laughing and joking with each other. Some were watching TV, and some had their siblings keeping them company while a nurse was distributing apple juice and crackers to all of them. I couldn't see any of them who were emotional. I asked the nurse if it was always like that, and she said yes—in fact, the nurses became attached to the patients as well, after having them for four to six months.

A social worker came to see me and extended any support I needed, like comfort for me and my family. I could call her anytime, she said, even during her off days, for any reason at all. She gave me some lists for support groups and a number for transportation problems.

The pharmacist introduced herself and explained the necessary medicine that would be prescribed to me during the chemotherapy treatment.

The Chemotherapy Cycle
I had been asked to bring my antinausea drugs with me, and to take them before the treatment. I also needed to take my antinausea drugs at home after therapy. It was easier to prevent nausea than to treat it once it occurred, so I followed directions closely.

Upon arriving at the clinic, I had to register at the reception so that they could order someone to check on my blood before the treatment. There was an "in and out" chart to determine if one was in the waiting area, and then I had to check my height and weight before waiting for my turn for treatment. This would be the routine for the next five cycles. I sat there wondering when my name would be called, because the waiting area was full. To occupy myself, I could watch TV, read a magazine or talk to people. I interviewed people sitting beside me and listened to their stories. For people who had some cycles done, I had heard what had happened to their cases, which was often more severe than what I had. I felt sad and would cry with them. When I heard that one of them and I had the same schedule, I thought I'd found a buddy. I took her number, and we eventually shared our experiences. The wait procedure and treatment lasted for three hours.

After my first treatment, when I arrived home, I took a rest and ate my dinner around six o'clock. By nine, I was continuously vomiting, and every time I drank water I threw it up. My system did not want to take anything, even though I had taken antinausea and antivomiting drugs. My husband had to bring me to the nearest hospital, and I was given an IV to avoid dehydration. Some effects that I encountered were fatigue (which they said was common, especially in the first week of treatment) and mouth sores on my tongue, gums, the sides of the mouth and in the throat, which made it difficult to swallow. I could hardly sleep because of dryness in my throat, and I had a headache as well. Every person could react differently on the regimen, and I was one of the people who reacted badly. I felt so frail for the first week, and my system was so picky on the food. When I felt well, I ate foods that relieved nausea, which my nutritionist had suggested. This was so strange that the foods that I used to like, I would like no more. My taste buds seemed to not work, and when I swallowed food, my stomach resisted. But there were foods that my stomach accepted, so those were the foods I ate, although they were not my favourites. I slowly regained my strength for two weeks, before the next treatment.

The second treatment was worse than the first one. There were sores on some delicate parts of my body, and one night I had such high blood pressure that my husband had to rush me to the emergency room. I had to visit the emergency room two times in my second cycle. I always said, "Not again," every time I was about to get the treatment.

Hair Loss

My hair fell out after three weeks; my scalp felt tender as well. My eyelashes and eyebrows fell out. This was the most horrible side effect of the regimen. This was the time that I would like to isolate myself from everybody, because I was physically and emotionally stressed. I worried about my appearance and felt anxious about my health, family and finances. Sometimes I wanted to mingle with other people, but aside from my immune system being low, my baldness would show my illness, and thus people felt and acted differently toward me. Even my kids reacted, although I explained to them what to expect while I was undergoing treatment. Still, it was different when they actually saw it, and they seemed to be alarmed. I could see the loneliness in their eyes and asked them how they felt. My two daughters seemed to understand, but my boy asked, "Are you dying?" I embraced him so hard and told him that losing hair was not dying; it was just the effect of the drug to treat my cancer. I assured them that I would be well.

I interviewed one of the patients who was bald to see if she socialized during treatment, and she answered yes, although she attended parties that were not so crowded and were more a family thing. I was given encouragement to socialize, so while I was regaining strength between treatments, I did attend some social functions, though I had to wear a wig. Most of the people could not tell that I was undergoing treatment.

Radiation/Cobalt

After my six-week cycle for chemotherapy, I had to rest for a month before starting radiation treatment. My doctor recommended I take a vacation before proceeding to this treatment, but I told him I wanted to get it over with and start right away. I was sent to Sunnybrook Hospital to do cobalt; I had to report there every day for eight weeks. It was not easy to travel there because I live 80 kilometres away, and traffic was brutal. There were trains or volunteer people who could pick up and drop off cancer patients, but only in certain areas. Sometimes my husband's schedule was not always favourable with mine, so I had to drive myself.

When I heard of radiation, the word seemed so scary. I was nervous on my first day, and I had lots of time to wonder because the waiting time was endless. On my turn, the technician instructed me to keep still while I was on the stretcher. I felt that I was the girl in the movie *Resident Evil* who was about to be experimented on. I was left alone in the room that had a heavy door just like a vault. Silence reigned for a few minutes, and then I heard the machine going across my left shoulder to the right. It was done for only five minutes, and the technician came in and told me it was complete!

I did not feel a thing; I thought I would feel at least a pinch of a ray from the radiation. It seemed like they did nothing on me, and it was a painless treatment, but as the day of treatment went on, the target area became darker and darker. I heard every person had a different skin reaction. I was lucky because my skin did not break or peel at all, until the end of the treatment. My doctor prescribed a nonmedicinal cream to apply on my skin if it broke. Even after four to six weeks of treatment, my radiation therapist told me that the treatment still was working on my system, so I should continue some of the special care around the area while undergoing treatment. I had not been advised to take any vitamins, but with a little research, I learned vitamins C, E and D were essential to take while in treatment.

Follow-up care depends on the type of cancer, how far the cancer has progressed at the time of diagnosis, how successful the radiation therapy was in treating the cancer, age and overall health. Schedule of follow-up visits is different for each person. My oncologist managed my follow-up care, and he also referred me back to my family doctor for routine check-ups.

The Drop

Coping
Support Group

I went to register to a support centre in Oshawa, which was called the Hearth Place; it had opened on Colborne Street in 1997. The place had been created by a breast cancer patient, Carolyn Alexander, who died shortly before it opened. The centre is the place for social, emotional and spiritual training for people dealing with all types of cancer.

The staff was so warm and friendly. The receptionist showed me the place and gave me the list of their programs and schedules. She recommended I register first for the "Look Good, Feel Better Program." This program was sponsored by different cosmetics companies. I signed in right away. The program boosted everyone's personality; I didn't feel alone when I was in that room. I felt I found sisters that had the same feathers as me. We could talk about ourselves freely. Everyone was given $200 worth of branded skin care and makeup, and we were taught techniques to apply makeup and how to take care of our skin while we were undergoing treatments. They taught us how to create turban or hair dress in economical ways, and how to use and care for human hair wigs and synthetic wigs. Most of all we were free to get hats that fit us well for free. It was fun.

I spent time looking for wigs, hats, scarves and turbans. I was addicted to it and didn't realize that I'd collected enough to wear different styles daily for a month. After a year, I am still into looking at different scarves, wigs and hats. I laughed because even my daughters were hunting for good hats for me every time they went shopping with their grandmother. A year later, I saw this beauty outlet store on Sheppard Avenue and Markham Road in Scarborough that had opened in summer 2011. I was so excited that they had different selections on wigs and hats. They had different beauty products and cost less compared to others. They had wigs on sale from time to time that cost $9.00 and up.

I also found a hair growth lotion in there that helped grow and thicken my hair. I did enjoy the store not just for the prices, but also because of their customer care. One time I asked my husband to pick a wig for me, and while he was there, he sent pictures via his phone of some styles. I told him to get one from the selection he sent. When he arrived home, I tried the wig, and it didn't look good on me. I understood that due to hygiene reasons, wigs were a final sale, but I went back to the store and tried to talk to them. I was entertained by Sue, and she was so considerate and understanding; she wrote off the wig and gave me another style that fit me. I offered a tip to her, but she declined. I cannot express how much I appreciated her gesture, and I definitely recommend this store to anyone to show my appreciation of her kindness. The address is 5085 Sheppard Ave E, unit 30.

Family

The best person who can be helping you is your partner. I knew my husband was also stressed, but he still had to tackle most of the job that I couldn't fulfil. I was so lucky to have a strong mom who supported me throughout, bought some groceries, cooked and helped with the household work at times like this. I was so thankful to have an energetic mother-in-law who bought my family groceries and cheered up my kids every weekend. My cousins and aunts abroad spiritually supported me as well.

Friends

I salute my best friend, who came to my house every time she was available and bought groceries. She cooked and she tidied up my house as well, without my requesting her to do it. Another friend of mine, whom I call Bes, lived across the globe, but distance was not a hindrance of support. Almost every day my Bes woke me up for some words of encouragement and prayers via e-mail and texts. Here were some messages he sent.

God's gift to us is people like you. With sincere prayers we whispered our thanks to him and ask him to bless you in ways only he can do. Have a great week.

Someday, everything that happens in our lives will make perfect sense, so for now let us laugh at the confusion, smile though the tears beneath and keep reminding ourselves that everything happens for a reason. Expect that out of our great troubles come our best blessing. Good day!

When we remember God's faithfulness and his ability to bring good out of any situation, we find our fears calmed and our confidence renewed. Whatever our worries today, don't be afraid; just stand where you are and watch the Lord strengthen and take care of you. God be with us always. Blessed Sunday!

Because you are special and wonderful, we pray that you be enriched by God's love and care, today and always. Good morning!

Those who faithfully bear the cross in this life will wear the crown in the life to come!

Heavenly father, thank you for the morning of my life. Make me see them as moments of rising and renewing of sharing, caring and bringing me even closer to you, Bless this day with your grace and mercy, amen. Joyful Thursday!

We have been created for a greater purpose. Don't let yourself fall into things that remove the beauty of your heart. Carry a heart that never hates. Carry a smile that never fades; carry a touch that never hurts. Be humble and carry love that always gives. Good morning!

And to all my friends all over the world: I won't forget the good gestures and prayers you extended to me.

While in treatment, most cancer victims are sometimes ashamed to ask for help, but we definitely need it. I suggest that if you know somebody who is close to you with cancer, do not hesitate to offer a hand—just do it and don't ask. It could be accompanying them to their doctor appointments, giving a ride, buying some groceries or giving cooked food, providing some help around their house and, if they have small kids, maybe babysitting for few hours.

AFTER THE RIDE

After all my treatments were done on December 1, 2010, I felt that my bones were weak. I could hardly open and close my hands, and my right middle finger was triggered. I often fell on my knees when I walked or jumped. My hip lock hurt when I got up from a sitting position, and my toes (bunion) hurt when I walked and wore shoes. Now that I had all these treatments, I asked myself, "What now?" When I visited my oncology doctor in February 2011, he told me that the weakness of my bones were the effect of chemotherapy. He referred me to a plastic surgeon regarding my trigger finger, and they did surgery on it. It was a minor surgery, but it was more difficult than when I had my mastectomy because it was my right hand, and being right handed I couldn't do much—even bathing myself, assisting my kids and many minor things were now difficult. The recovery time last for six weeks, and I became impatient. The pain on my joints would get better in time, I was told, but it'd been 10 months, and I still felt some difficulty in standing up from kneeling or seating, and I also had some twitching in my fingers and neck. I wondered if I was the only one having this problem, so I did not want to mention it because people might think that I was just overacting. I did research and was relieved that there were people who did experience joint pain, even 24 months after their last treatment.

I saw my oncology doctor every three months as he required. I had to see my medical surgeon every year and do tests, in order to monitor for any radicals that may come back. My oncology doctor told me that it would take another five years to see whether all my cells came back as good cells. A hormonal therapy pills was prescribed for me to take for five years to get better. I had a negative notion about this therapy, so I laid it out to my doctor. He said that this prescribed pills would make me well. He was the expert on this kind of illness, so I followed through.

Reconstruction

When I woke up in the morning, I didn't feel right every time I saw my image in the mirror. My feelings would never be the same; I felt like my womanhood was taken away. Because of the complication during my first surgery, I had a big diamond scar on my stomach and a diagonal scar on my chest. I told myself I would definitely have a reconstruction done, but I had to wait at least one year to heal my chest from radiation before it could be done. For a year, I felt incomplete even if I wore prosthetic bras (which were pricey, by the way). I felt so unattractive and described myself as Frankenstein, although this scar symbolized a great warrior and survivor battling cancer. I went to see my plastic surgeon three times to ask whether reconstruction was possible, but she said if my chest was not healed, then once my chest opened my bones would collapse and more problems would arise. There

26

were several types of reconstruction, which my plastic surgeon explained to me earlier, and I researched them as well.

Breast reconstruction is a procedure to rebuild a breast's shape. It's an option for most women after mastectomy. Reconstruction was not popular in the eighties, but now more and more women take the option, depending on their situation. Some survivors were hesitant to perform this because they just didn't want that knife to slice their body again. Some had fear because of a lack of information. Some took two years or more to think about it before deciding to proceed.

There were different methods of reconstruction, which my plastic surgeon explained to me, and some readings also enlightened me. A good understanding and the right information will help you decide what type you prefer. If a nipple and areola have been removed, it is also possible to have them reconstructed using tissue from other areas of your body, or sometimes tattooing.

The two main types of breast reconstruction have different techniques.

The most common implant is a shell filled with saline (sterile salt water) or silicone gel. It is placed under the skin and muscle of the chest wall.

If the skin and chest wall tissues are tight and flat, you may need the tissue-expansion method of implant. With this method, an expander implant (an empty bag with a small valve, like a balloon) is placed under the skin and muscle of the chest wall. Small amounts of saline are injected into the shell's valve, using a very small needle inserted through the skin. Many visits to the doctor are needed to stretch the skin and fully expand the breast implant to the size of the opposite breast. After the skin has stretched enough, the expander implant is usually removed in a second operation, and a permanent implant is put in its place. Sometimes expander implants are left in place as the final implant. I was amazed when my doctor told me that some women make an appointment on the day of the party they are going to attend, to increase their breast size. This type is very flexible to increase and decrease the size that you want.

This kind of implant is a simple technique. You can have it done as an outpatient, meaning you won't need to stay overnight at the hospital.

The possible side effects with breast implants are:

1. Infection

2. Implant getting hard over time and the breast losing its shape

3. Scar tissue forming around the implant

4. Small risk of leak or rupture

The other type is the tissue flap techniques. In tissue flap techniques, a section of skin and fat (and often muscle) is moved from the abdomen, back or other area of the body to the chest area, to shape a breast. The different tissue flap techniques are as follows.

A. Tram Flap
Skin, fat and muscle (with its own blood supply) from the lower abdomen are tunnelled under the skin up to the chest to form a breast. The advantage of this

technique is that the reconstructed breast is made of natural tissue and has a more natural feel than an implant.

The possible side effects of tram flap technique include:

1. Scars on your abdomen and on the reconstructed breast, which never completely go away

2. Infection and bleeding after surgery

3. Build-up of fluid where the tissue was taken

4. Longer operation and recovery time than implant

5. The tissue in the area not surviving if there is a poor blood supply to the reconstructed breast

B. Lats Flap
Skin, fat and muscle (with its own blood supply) from the upper back are tunnelled under the skin and turned to the front to form a breast. An implant is added in women who need a larger breast.

The reconstructed breast has natural tissue covering the implant (when used) and has a more natural feel. This technique also adds fullness to the lower part of the breast, where it is most needed to produce a natural-looking breast.

The possible problems or side effects of lats flap technique include:

1. Scars on your back and on the reconstructed breast, which never completely go away

2. Infection and bleeding after surgery

3. Build-up of fluid where the tissue was taken

4. Skin taken from the back being a different colour and texture than skin in the breast area

5. Longer operation and recovery time than implant surgery

6. Less muscle strength on the side after surgery

7. The tissue in the area not surviving if there is a poor blood supply to the reconstructed breast

C. Free Flap
Skin, fat, muscle and blood vessels are removed from one area of the body (for example, the abdomen or buttocks) and placed under the skin on the chest to create a breast. The free flap method isn't used very often and needs a plastic surgeon who is skilled in microsurgery to reconnect tiny blood vessels to the flap in the new breast location. The advantage of the free flap method is that more of the muscle is left in place that with other flap methods, which may mean that strength can be recovered faster.

Possible problems or side effects of the free flap technique are the same as other flap techniques. There is also more scarring in the area where the flap is taken.

D. Diep Flap
Skin, fat and blood vessels, but not muscle, are removed from the abdomen and placed under the skin on the chest to form a breast. This method isn't used very often and needs a plastic surgeon who is skilled in microsurgery to reconnect the tiny blood vessels to

the flap in the new breast location. The advantage of the Diep flap method is that the muscle is left in place, which may mean that strength can be recovered faster.

Possible problems or side effects of the Diep flap technique are the same as other flap techniques. There is also more scarring in the area where the flap is taken.

Without hesitation I had my reconstruction late in 2011, and I now feel magically complete and beautiful. I am so happy that I did it, and I definitely recommend it for breast cancer victims who qualify. It makes a big difference and builds your confidence.

On October 17, 2012, I was invited to the Scarborough Hospital to celebrate Breast Reconstruction Awareness Day (BRA). BRA day is introduced to promote education, awareness and access for women to consider breast reconstruction after mastectomy as part of a treatment. The event is successful, and experienced surgeons explain and educate people about reconstruction through the use of microsurgery, showing video on how it was done. The presentations are done in English, Chinese and Tamil. During break time, everyone is free to talk to the surgeons, walk around and even peek in the microscope and feel implants while enjoying the lovely cupcakes, chocolates and sandwiches. I was amazed what the surgeons do! Scarborough Hospital has the busiest operating rooms in the province annually.

Maintenance

According to Health Canada, modifying one's lifestyle,

31

observing eating habits and getting active will reduce or prevent cancer. I am now in a habit of reading anything about nutrition, which I believe plays an important role in my recovery.

What is cancer, anyway? It is in fact a disease that begins in our cells. We have tons of cells that somehow form in a group, and they become tissues and organs and muscles and bones. The process of genes in each cell command it to grow, work, reproduce and die. The cells normally remain behaved. But somehow the cells get mixed up in the gene's command, and they become abnormal cells; then they develop a lump, or tumour. Tumours can either be benign, which are noncancerous, or malignant, which are cancerous. Benign tumour cells stay in one place in the body and are not usually life threatening. Malignant tumour cells are able to invade nearby tissues and spread to other parts of the body. When cancer cells travel to other parts of the body, it is called metastasis.

The first sign that a malignant tumour has spread or metastasized is often swelling of nearby lymph nodes, but cancer can spread to almost any part of the body. It is best to find and treat malignant tumours as early as possible. Be sure to have a regular check-up with your family doctor. I had received lots of information regarding fruits and vegetables that fight diseases from e-mail, friends and the news, and I was thankful that they were feeding me information that they thought would be good for me, as a sign of their love and care. You have probably received the same information regarding asparagus, soursop, all berries and the proper ways of eating them (e.g., fruits should be eaten on an empty stomach), green tea cures, honey and cinnamon.

These are good but can lead to confusion. I decided to research foods that fight, which will be enumerated in the next pages under "Food That Has 'It.'" I felt the difference when I ate lots of fruits and vegetables, and I am proud and happy to share my tips to everyone.

In my research, some habits that might cause cancer are stress, eating unhealthy food (i.e., processed food, too many sweet or fried foods), less sleep and no exercise. As they say, if you do the same thing over and over again, the result will always be the same. I did assess myself on what I had been doing before diagnosis. I felt guilty because I abused myself. I am active only for work. I deprived myself of sleeping, and I ate unhealthy food. I love fast food; one of my favourites is French fries. I snack on chips a lot and always have cookies on my desk, and I munch popcorn with nuts. However, all those yummy things are killer. Now I believe it is not too late to change my eating habit and be fit once again. Truly I entertain any information about anything that helps me be well. I read all electronically transmitted messages coming from friends, relatives and colleagues, but I have to dig into how factual the information is.

FOOD THAT HAS "IT"

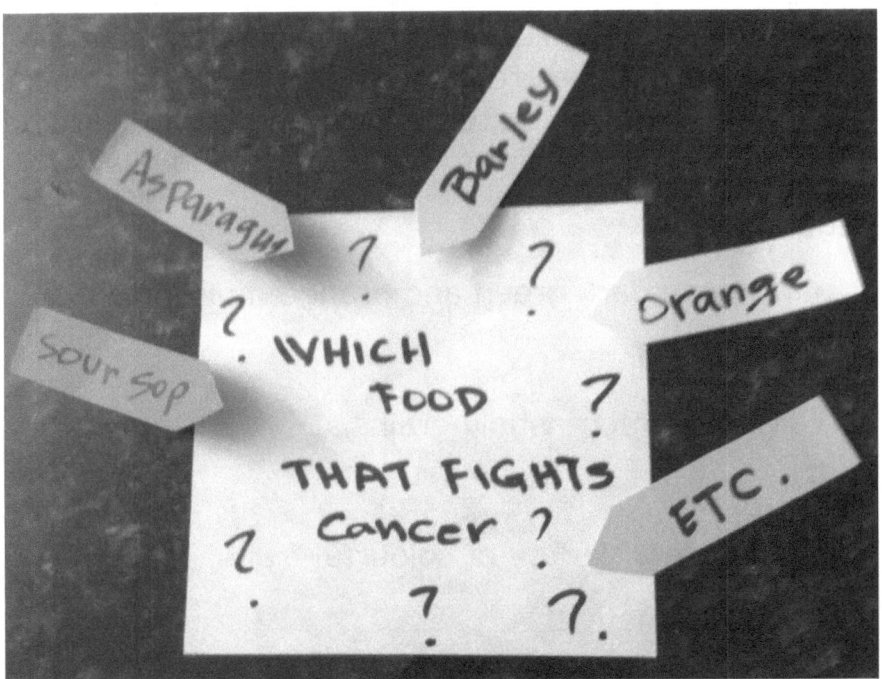

Asparagus, barley, green tea, blueberries, sour sop, fish instead of meat, etc.

All of the foods in the picture will contribute something good to our body, but a balanced diet is the key. It is time to review our basic food groups.

Food Guide to Healthy Eating

Different people need different amounts of food. This guide gives you a lower and higher number of servings from each food group. See a dietician to help you determine how much you need for better results.

In a simple sense, as the circle of the rainbow narrows, a smaller amount of food intake should be the goal. The outer circle has the most amount, where lay the vegetables, and the second circle belongs to the grains and starches. Those are followed by the fruits, smaller quantities of milk and alternatives, and then meat and alternatives. The smallest intake is fats and oils.

Vegetables

- Choose dark green and orange more often.

Grains and Starches

- Choose more whole grains.

Fruits

- Choose a variety of colourful fruits.

Milk and Alternatives

- Choose lower fat dairy products.

Meat and Alternatives

- Choose lean meats, poultry, fish and beans.

Fats and Oils

- Choose fats from nuts and vegetable oils.

If you want a quick answer and ask me, "What are the

best fruits and vegetables that should be eaten?" then my answer is go for the rainbow, which means eat a variety of fruit and vegetables in different colours. All of them will contribute vitamins and minerals to the body.

Recommended Daily Food Choices

Sources:
- Health Canada, Canada's Food Guide, http://www.hc-sc.gc.ca

- The Diabetes Food Guide to Healthy Eating, 2009, The Community Diabetes Education Program of Ottawa

Vegetables
5+ choices a day

- 1 cup raw leafy greens: spinach, romaine, kale, endive

- 1/2 cup raw or cooked: asparagus, beets, broccoli, green and yellow string beans, carrots, cabbage, cauliflower, celery, cucumber, eggplant, leeks, mushrooms, mixed frozen vegetables, onions, green and red peppers, tomato, turnips, zucchini

Note: portions of more than one cup of parsnips, peas, winter squash and tomato sauce will add 15 grams of available carbohydrate (3 teaspoons of sugar) to your meal.

Carbohydrates
1 choice from carbohydrate foods = 15 grams of carbohydrate (3 teaspoons of sugar)

- 45–60 grams of carbohydrates is a meal
- 15–20 grams of carbohydrates is a snack

Grains and Starches
6–8 choices a day

(Measure after cooking)

1 slice whole grain bread	1/2 medium potato	1/2 (6") Pita bread
3/4 cup hot cereal	1/2 cup mashed potato	1/4 large bagel
1/2 cup cold cereal	1/3 cup brown rice, white rice, millet	1(4") pancake or waffle
1/2 cup barley, bulgur	1 (2") small muffin	1/3 cup sweet potato
Buckwheat, corn, wild rice	1 (6") whole wheat chapatti, roti, tortilla	3 cups popcorn
1/2 cup pasta, couscous		

Fruits
3 choices a day

1 medium apple, orange, pear	1 large peach, nectarine	15 grapes, cherries
2 cups strawberries, blackberries, raspberries	1/2 cup unsweetened applesauce, canned	2 medium kiwi, plums, clementine oranges
1 cup blueberries	1/2 cup unsweetened juice	1/2 medium mango
1 cup melon	1/4 cup dried fruit	1 small banana, grapefruit

Milk and Alternatives
2–3 choices a day

1 cup milk	1/2 cup flavoured soy beverage	1/2 cup evaporated milk
1 cup plain soy beverage	4 Tbsp powdered milk	3/4 cup plain low-fat yogurt

Meat and Alternatives
4–8 choices a day

(Measure after cooking)

1 ounce (30 g) lean meat	1/4 cup cottage cheese (1–2% milk fat)
Poultry or fish	1 ounce (30 g) cheese (<20% milk fat)
1 large egg	1/2 cup legumes (beans, peas, lentils)
1/2 block (85 g) tofu	1/3 cup hummus

*portions of more than ½ cup of beans and lentils will add 15 grams of available carbohydrate (3 teaspoons of sugar) to your meal.

Fats and Oils
In moderation

1 tsp margarine, nonhydrogenated	1 Tbsp nuts or seeds
1 tsp oil (canola, olive or peanut)	1 Tbsp salad dressing, regular
1 Tbsp mayonnaise, light	1 slice bacon

Sweets
Have sweets in moderation and enjoy small portions. Choose food and beverages low in added sugars.

Plan Your Healthy Meal

The American Institute Cancer Research recommends people consume two-third or more of their meal in plant food such as vegetables, fruits, whole grain and beans, to reduce the risk of cancer. Check it out: http://www.foodproductdesign.com.

Reminder: Fruits and vegetables are not a substitute for medicine in treating diseases and illnesses. Have a regular checkup and consult your health-care team. The key is to listen to your body; do not compare your situation to another individual's. Everyone has a different situation.

By using the recommended daily food intake for healthy eating, you could enjoy eating planned snacks or meals. Remember to eat more vegetables because they are very high in nutrients and low in calories. Choose starch foods such as whole grain breads and cereals, rice, noodles or potatoes at every meal. Starch foods are broken down into glucose, which your body needs for energy. Include fish, lean meats, low-fat cheeses, eggs or vegetarian protein choices as part of your meal. Have a glass of milk and a piece of fruit to complete your meal. Talk to your doctor about how much is safe to include alcohol in your meal plan.

Sometimes it is hard to remember the daily food intake guide, and it varies to every individual. Here is another handy portion guide, which I prefer more than the "medium plate guide" that I mentioned earlier. The hands can be very useful in estimating appropriate portions. Every individual has a different size, so your own hands more accurately measure your portion.

Vegetables

Choose as much as you can hold in both hands. Here are some powerful vegetables on my list.

Asparagus

Asparagus is popular as one food that fights cancer. It is used to treat rheumatism, gout and cystitis because of its combination of anti-inflammatory nutrients. It also has very impressive results from several studies due to being high in antioxidants, which include vitamin C, beta carotene, vitamin E, zinc, manganese and selenium. If you lack enzymes to break down asparagines, it produces urine with strong odour, a disconcerting but harmless phenomenon.

Asparagus is commonly sold by the bundle and displays at the grocery upright, often sitting in a watered container. You must select a bright green colour with close, compact, firm tips; most of the green colour should cover most of the spear. Stalks should be green in colour far down. You might want to buy stalks that are almost the same thickness, for even cooking. Avoid spears that are spread out, are moulding or have decayed tips—those are sign of aging, tough and poor asparagus. You may soak in cold water to freshen them up. You may store the asparagus bundles by setting them on a tray with at least one inch of water and put in your refrigerator. Cook it within two to three days.

Beets

Recent research has shown that drinking at least one glass of raw beet juice a day helps control cancer and prevents diarrhea. During early times, beets were used as a medicine; as a blood tonic for gastritis, piles and constipation; and as a mild cardio-tonic.

Broccoli

Broccoli is one of the good veggies. It is a cruciferous vegetable, which means it has a high concentration of the cancer-fighting chemicals known as glucosinolates. It's good to eat raw, steamed or in a stir fry. It is high in beta carotene, vitamin C, folic acid and iron, and it has a moderate level of calcium.

Carrots

According to an article in *Natural News* by Jonathan Benson on October 23, 2010, eating food that is rich in beta carotene slows cancerous growths. Carrots are extremely rich in beta carotene (vitamin A) and have small amounts of vitamin E.

Carrots are reputed to be therapeutic against asthma, general nervousness, dropsy and skin disorder. Carrot juice is noted to prevent diarrhea. Carrots are also good sources of fibre, vitamin C and potassium.

Cauliflower

This is also reputed for reducing the risk of cancer, especially for the colon and stomach.

Chinese Cabbage

Also known as Napa cabbage or celery cabbage, Chinese cabbage has moderate folic acid and vitamin C levels. It helps to reduce the risk of cancer.

Cook Chinese cabbage only lightly, to retain the flavour and nutrients. It is noted that to minimize the risk of listeria, you should never store Chinese cabbage in a plastic bag.

Kale

This cruciferous vegetable is one that I used to ignore every time I saw it in the grocery store. I hadn't heard of the nutrients that one can get, until I started searching for the best vegetables and fruits to fight cancer. Like collards, broccoli and cauliflower, kale is a descendent of wild cabbage; it originated in Asia. It has recently become popular due to its health-promoting, sulfur-containing phytonutrients. Kale is available in some markets year round, but the best and most abundant is from the middle of winter through the beginning of spring.

It has been said that kale supports the body's detoxification processes. The isothiocyanates (ITCs) made from kale's glucosinolates have been helpful to regulate detox activities in cells. Toxins that are risking our body must be detoxified by our cells in two steps, which are phase I and phase II detoxification. The ITC and sulfur compounds in kale support aspects of phase II detoxification. Kale has an important role in dealing with toxic exposure, whether the toxin is from the environment or from food intake.

Include this in your regular diet to have fantastic health benefits. You may have one and a half to two cups per meal, three times a week.

Did you know that kale is a good snack? Wash the leaves in running water, take off the stem, pat dry, and bake it for 10–15 minutes at 350°F, or take it out when it is crisp. My kids love the natural flavour and the taste.

Lettuce
Lettuces are annually grown for edible leaves year round. There are three categories of this vegetable: head lettuce (including butterhead types and crisphead), loose leaf (iceberg has very crisp, tender leaves) and romaine. They are very rich in beta carotene, especially the outer leaves.

They have many medicinal uses, like a mild sedative and narcotic. Lettuce soup is reported to be effective in treating nervous tension and insomnia. It could be a pain killer when the sap is dissolved in wine. It could also soothe inflammation. If extracted, you could use it as a lotion to treat your sunburn and rough skin. It can be used as poultice on bruises. It can be used to soothe coughs and bronchial problems, as well as stomach ulcers and irritable bowel syndrome.

Malunggay (also known as Moringa Oleifera)
This vegetable is not known to many, but it has been promoted by the World Health Organization (WHO) for the past 20 years to poor countries around the world as a "miracle vegetable" because it is a low-cost enhancer and is high in nutrients.

Malunggay is very rich in vitamin C, and it is very good as one of the four dietary antioxidants that the US Drug Administration recognizes. A dietary oxidant is a substance that is present in the food that helps to decrease the unfavourable effects of harmful chemicals.

It has four times the vitamin A in carrots, two times the protein in milk and the potassium found in banana, as well as iron and a high density of lipoprotein, or good cholesterol. Because of its high calcium content, which is four times the calcium in milk, mothers who breastfeed consume more malunggay leaves to produce more milk. The leaves are similar to spinach, and you can toss them in a salad, steam them, mix them with pancakes, make a soup or simply boil and drink it like a tea.

I personally buy this vegetable frozen in the Chinese grocery store or in any Asian store.

Pumpkin and Squash

Squash is another vegetable that is said to reduce the risk of cancer. It is high in beta carotene, with moderate amounts of vitamin C and folic acid. Seeds from squashes are used as a laxative and purgative in Ethiopia. They are also used worldwide to expel intestinal worms.

Spinach

This green is full of nutrients. It used to be well-known to kids that if Popeye eats spinach, he becomes strong and has bigger muscles; this story should be revived and told to your kids, and they will likely want to eat spinach more. There are many recipes that you can serve to your kids. You may mix it with pancakes or lasagne, or toss it into a salad. Spinach is high in iron, beta carotene and folic acid; it is also rich in vitamins A and C.

Sweet Peppers and Hot Peppers

These peppers are annuals and short-lived perennials, grown for edible fruits that are very rich in vitamin C and beta carotene. They have been said to help the body metabolize alcohol, act as an expectorant and prevent and alleviate bronchitis and emphysema. If you drink a glass of water daily with 10–20 drops of red-hot chili sauce (or if you eat spicy meals 3 times a week), it can keep airways free of congestion, preventing or treating chronic bronchitis and colds. It also stimulates endorphins, killing pain and inducing a sense of well-being.

Freshest Produce

Fruits and vegetables are at their best when they are fresh. The freshest you can get is from your backyard or to buy locally produced ones. These produce are picked when they are fully ripe and ready for the grocery stores. This means they are more nutritious, which is good for your health, is good for the environment and is the right choice to support farmers in your area.

Imported produce are picked weeks before they are ripe, and often the nutrients, taste, texture and colours have not fully developed. When a vegetable is harvested, after 24–48 hours it has been said that 50–89 percent of the vitamin C is lost. Bagged spinach loses half its folate and carotenoids after being stored in the refrigerator for just four days. Imported produce from other countries lose about the same nutrients.

Organic versus Locally Grown Produce

It is now common in grocery stores to have produce labelled organic. Organic food is grown with environmentally friendly agricultural methods. In order to be labelled as organic, the farms must meet a certain government standard. But when these produce travel long distances to market (which is called food miles), it creates pollution that sometimes outweighs the positive environmental effects of organic farming—and you still lose some nutrients.

Locally grown produce are fresh because they do not have food miles. It helps a community's economy and reduces environmental cost associated with food miles. However, local food is not necessarily grown with organic methods.

Grains and Starches

Research published in the October 2004 issue of *Nutrition and Metabolism* demonstrated that 5.4 percent of the carbohydrate content in a meal with resistant starch significantly increases lipid oxidation in adult subjects. Resistant starch could help people burn more fat and speed up metabolism.

One of the researchers on resistant starch (RS), Dr. Higgins, says, "The RS actually changes the order in which the body burns food. Usually carbohydrates are used first, but resistant starch seems to move fat to the top of the list to be burned for energy before it has a chance to be stored."

Here are some carbs that reduce cancer and that are fat-burning foods. Choose an amount the size of your fist for each of the grains and starches.

Banana
Bananas have a generally known shape with a remarkable scent, and they are the most productive food crop. Bananas are rich in starch and low in saturated fat, cholesterol and sodium. They're a good source of dietary fibre, vitamin C and potassium.

Barley

Barley is a member of the grass family and is a type of cereal. Barley has a nut flavour, has a spectacular chewy texture and is rich in fibre. Just for the fibre alone, it has a lot of healthy benefits.

In our body process, somehow the friendly bacteria ferment insoluble fibre, and they produce a short-chain fatty acid called butyric acid, which serves as primary fuel for cells of the large intestine and helps a healthy colon. There are two other fatty acids that were created: propionic acid (which may be partly responsible for the cholesterol-lowering properties of fibre) and acetic acid. Both acids are used as fuel by the liver and the muscles.

The Archives of Internal Medicine confirms that eating high-fibre foods such as barley helps prevent heart disease. Fibre in barley can also prevent blood sugar levels from rising too high in people with diabetes.

Surprisingly, barley has a variety of uses. Malting barley is used to make beverages like beer and whiskey. It is used as sweeteners in a variety of foods. Noodles, cereals and instant baby formulas are made from barley. It's also used to feed hogs, cattle and poultry.

Here are some different dishes that I love to prepare. The recipes with their nutrients come from the National Barley Foods Council (http://www.barleyfoods.org).

Breakfast
Barley Orange Pancakes

1 cup barley flour

1/3 cup all-purpose flour

1/4 cup granulated sugar (could be omitted for diabetics)

2 teaspoons baking powder

1/2 teaspoon baking soda

1 cup part skim milk ricotta cheese

1/2 cup 2% milk

1/2 cup orange juice

1 teaspoon grated orange peel

2 large eggs, beaten

3 tablespoons butter, melted

1 teaspoon vanilla

Warm syrup and butter for toppings

1. In a large bowl, combine flours, sugar, baking powder and baking soda; set aside.

2. In another bowl, beat together ricotta, milk, orange juice, orange peel, eggs, butter and vanilla.

3. Mix liquid ingredients into dry ingredients until well blended.

4. Heat griddle or frying pan until hot.

5. Spray with nonstick cooking spray.

6. Spoon about 3 tablespoons batter onto griddle.

7. Cook pancake until bubbles appear.

8. Turn and cook until golden brown.

9. Serve with warm syrup and butter.

10. Make 12 pancakes.

Nutrients per serving (2 pancakes): calories 262, protein 10 g, carbohydrates 32 g, fibre 2 g, fat 12 g, cholesterol 101 mg, sodium 409 mg.

Salad
Teriyaki Barley Salad

1/2 cup pearl barley or whole grain barley

1 1/2 cups water

1/4 teaspoon salt (could be omitted)

2 medium carrots, thinly sliced

1/2 pound snow peas

2 cups cooked and cubed chicken

1 can (8 ounces) sliced water chestnuts, drained

4 green onions, sliced

1/4 cup vegetable oil

1/4 cup prepared teriyaki sauce

1 tablespoon white wine vinegar

1 teaspoon grated fresh ginger or 1/4 teaspoon ground ginger

1/2 teaspoon garlic powder

1. Bring water to a boil in medium saucepan with lid.

2. Add barley and return to boil, reduce heat, cover and cook 45 minutes (if using whole grain barley, 50–55 minutes), or until tender and liquid is absorbed. Pour off any unabsorbed liquid.

3. Cook carrots in boiling water for 5 minutes.

4. Add snow peas and cook 1 minute.

5. Rinse cooked vegetable and drain.

6. Combine cooked barley, cooked vegetables, chicken, water chestnuts and green onions.

7. Pour over barley salad and mix well.

8. Cover salad and refrigerate until chilled.

Makes 6 servings.

Per serving: calories 288, protein 18 g, fat 13 g, carbohydrates 26 g, cholesterol 41 mg, fibre 5 g, sodium 616 mg.

Main Dish
Fillet of Sole with Barley and Asparagus

1 cup pearl barley

3 cups water

1 can (14 1/2 ounces) diced tomatoes and juice

1 tablespoon Italian seasoning

4 fresh sole fillets, about 12 ounces (defrost if using frozen fillets)

1 tablespoon fresh lemon juice

12 fresh asparagus spears, trimmed to 6 inches in length and blanched (defrost if using frozen asparagus)

1/3 cup low-fat mayonnaise

2 tablespoons chopped green onion

2 tablespoons Dijon-style mustard

2 tablespoons grated fresh Parmesan cheese

1. Bring barley to a boil and cook until tender, or about 45 minutes.

2. Combine cooked barley, tomatoes and juice and Italian seasoning. Place in 11×7×2 inch baking dish.

3. Sprinkle each sole fillet with lemon juice. Place 3 asparagus spears in centre of each fillet and roll up.

4. Arrange rolled fillets on top of barley, seam-side down. Set aside.

5. Combine mayonnaise, green onion and mustard in a small bowl.

6. Spoon sauce over fillets and sprinkle with Parmesan cheese.

7. Bake in preheated 350°F oven for 25 minutes, or until sole flakes easily with fork.

8. Makes 4 servings.

Per serving: calories 390, protein 26 g, fat 11 g, carbohydrates 51 g, cholesterol 41 mg, fibre 16 g, sodium 592 mg.

Scones
Barley Fruit Scones

1 cup barley flour

1 cup all-purpose wheat flour

1/4 cup granulated sugar (you could omit for diabetics)

1 tablespoon baking powder

1/2 teaspoon salt

1/2 cup dried cranberries (you may use currants, raisins or dried cherries)

1 cup nonfat milk

1/4 cup butter, melted

1 large egg, beaten

1 teaspoon grated fresh lemon peel

Lemon Glaze

1/4 cup confectioner's sugar, sifted

1 teaspoon grated fresh lemon peel

1 tablespoon fresh lemon juice

1. Mix together powdered ingredients in a large bowl.

2. Stir in cranberries.

3. Mix all remaining ingredients.

4. Spray a baking sheet with nonstick cooking spray.

5. Drop batter by spoonful onto baking sheet, creating 12 equal portions.

6. Bake at 375°F for 15–17 minutes, or until lightly browned.

7. Cool scones slightly. Combine lemon glaze ingredients; stir until smooth. Use pastry brush to glaze tops of cooled scones.

8. Make 12 scones.

Per scone: calories 178, protein 4 g, carbohydrates 31 g, fat 5 g, fibre 2 g, cholesterol 28 mg, sodium 276 mg.

Barley Fruit Muffins
1 1/2 cups all-purpose flour

1/2 cup barley flour

2 teaspoons baking powder

1 teaspoon ground cinnamon

1/2 teaspoon salt

1 cup (8 ounces) low-fat vanilla yogurt

2 eggs

2/3 cup dark brown sugar, packed

1/4 cup light olive oil

1 teaspoon vanilla extract

1/4 cup chopped dried fruit (apricots, apples, raisins, cranberries or cherries)

1. Whisk all remaining ingredients (do not include brown sugar yet) in a large bowl; set aside.

2. Whisk all remaining ingredients together until smooth in a medium bowl.

3. Pour into dry ingredients, mixing until just combined.

4. Stir in dried fruit.

5. Bake with nonstick 12-cup muffin tin in preheated 375°F oven for 15–18 minutes, or until toothpick inserted in centre comes out clean.

6. Cool in pan in 10 minutes; turn muffins out onto cooling rack.

7. Makes 12 muffins.

Per muffin: 199 calories, 4 g protein, 34 g carbohydrate, 2 g fibre, 6 g fat, 36 mg cholesterol, 260 mg sodium.

Beans

Beans are also known as legumes, and they include lentils, peas and soybeans. They are a great source of fibre and therefore contribute to fighting some cancers, as well as preventing high blood pressure and cholesterol.

Soybean

Soy: Tofu, Tempeh, Edamame, Soymilk, Miso

The soybean is very rich in phytoestrogen hormones

called isoflavones. Isoflavones are polyphenolic compounds that are capable of exerting an estrogen-like effect, and adding soybean to your diet increases estrogen levels. The American Institute for Cancer Research (AICR), which provides funding for research to leading universities, hospitals and research centres in the United States and abroad, says that there was a fear that soy may increase the risk of hormone-related cancer, but evidence shows this is not true. The fears were a result of rodent studies. Scientists now know that rodents and most other laboratory animals metabolize soy isoflavones differently than humans. Soy consumption does not lead to increased estrogen levels in humans. Soy does not increase a breast cancer survivor's risk of recurrence or death. Wendy Chen, MD, MPH, says that soy should be taken regularly as part of our diet, but select dietary soy, not processed soy or in pill form. We should also not to eat soy exclusively. Women who ate a large amount of soy have decreased breast cancer recurrence compared to women who do not eat soy.

A ganistein compound is present in soybean and is a possible anticancer agent. It appears to be able to interfere at the production of these protective proteins and could reduce the ability of cancer cells to grow.

Most people use soybean oil for salad, but you are not getting enough nutrients by that alone.

Here are two recipes that my kids love to bake and eat. The recipes come from http://www.tofurecipesonsoyfood.com.

Easy Lasagne
1 can (8 oz) mushrooms, chopped

1 1/2 cups zucchini, chopped

1 package (16 oz) water-packed, firm tofu, drained

1 Tablespoon lemon juice

1 Tablespoon dried parsley flakes

1 teaspoon Italian herb seasoning

1/4 teaspoon black pepper

3/4 cup water

4 cups fat-free marinara sauce

1 package (8 oz) lasagne noodles, uncooked

1 package (8 oz) mozzarella-style soy cheese, grated

1/4 cup Parmesan-style soy cheese

1. Preheat oven to 350°F.

2. Cook the mushrooms and zucchini in a nonstick skillet until tender, adding a little water if needed; set aside.

3. Mash the tofu in a small mixing bowl; add the lemon juice, dried parsley flakes, Italian herb seasoning and pepper; mix well.

4. Combine the water and marinara sauce. (The extra water will be absorbed by the uncooked noodles.)

5. Assemble the lasagne. Put about 1/3 of the sauce on the bottom of a 9×13 baking dish. Top with half the uncooked noodles, half the tofu mixture, half the mozzarella-style soy cheese and all the mushrooms and zucchini.

6. Put another 1/3 of the sauce on top the remaining noodles, the remaining tofu and then the last 1/3 of the sauce.

7. Top this with the remaining mozzarella-style and Parmesan-style soy cheeses.

8. Cover the casserole with foil.

9. Bake at 350°F for one hour.

10. Remove from oven and let sit 10–15 minutes to make serving easier.

11. Makes 9 servings.

Per serving: 235 calories, 5 g total fat (1 g sat fat), 0 mg cholesterol, 496 mg sodium, 32 g carbohydrate, 15 g protein (5 g soy protein), 3 g dietary fibre.

Cheesy Tofu Potato Casserole
10 medium potatoes

1 package (12 oz) silken firm tofu

1/2 cup soymilk (plain or vanilla)

1/2 teaspoon salt

1/4 cup sour cream (regular or soy)

3 cups shredded cheddar cheese

1. Peel and cook potatoes in water for mashing.

2. Blend silken tofu and soymilk in the blender until smooth.

3. Place cooked potatoes into 4-quart mixer; blend on low while adding soymilk tofu mixture. Add salt

to potato, tofu and soymilk mixture. Optional: for additional flavour, 1/2 cup of finely chopped leeks or green onions can be added while blending.

4. Continue blending on low-medium speed until potatoes are smooth.

5. Layer half of potatoes in 3-quart Pyrex pan.

6. Spread a layer of cheese over top to fill half the pan.

7. Spread remainder of potatoes over cheese.

8. Spread remainder of cheese over potatoes.

9. Bake at 350°F for 15 minutes, until cheese is melted.

10. Sprinkle bacon bits on top of mixture.

11. Makes 8 servings.

Per serving: 303 calories, 17.2 g fat (9 g sat fat), 48 mg cholesterol, 409 mg sodium, 22.5 g carbohydrate, 15.5 g protein (2.4 g soy protein), 2.1 g dietary fibre.

Brown Rice
Every rice grain has an outer cover, which is called the husk. If partially milled, rice has a thin brown layer retained on the grain; it is called the "bran," and the grain is brown. If milled fully, then the grain becomes white. The brown grain is more nutritional compared to white grain. The grain is rich in fibre because of the bran, low in saturated fat, very low in cholesterol and sodium and also a good source of selenium. Fibre content has a major role in our body system: it helps

digestion, reduces constipation, controls sugar levels and reduces the possibility of heart disease.

Be sure to check the manufacturing date when buying brown rice, because it becomes stale or gives a rancid flavour within four to five months. The light brown colour of the grain has a natural oil that causes the rancid flavour.

Sweet Corn
According to an assistant professor of food science at Cornell University and the lead author of the article "Processed Sweet Corn Has Higher Antioxidant Activity" in the August 14, 2002, issue of *Journal of Agriculture and Food Chemistry*, cooking sweet corn reduces the chance of cancer and heart disease. Cooked sweet corn retains antioxidant activity. Aside from antioxidant benefits, corn releases a phenolic compound called ferulic acid, which provides health benefits such as cancer-fighting properties.

Potatoes
Surprisingly, potatoes have many nutrients for the amount of calories they have. The fibre is half-soluble and helps to lower cholesterol, slowing down digestion and keeping you full longer because of the phytochemicals in them, including flavoids and kuloamine (which is a recently identified compound that appears to lower blood pressure). Potatoes are high in potassium, vitamin A, iron and copper. Potato is rich with vitamin C, but normally this is not eaten raw, so because of the heat in cooking, the vitamin C benefit is lessened.

Sweet Potato
Also known as kumara, Louisiana yam and yellow

yam, the sweet potato is an excellent source of beta carotene, is rich in carbohydrate and has moderate potassium and vitamins B and C. Yellow and orange types are rich in vitamin C. Sweet potatoes and their leaves contain antibacterial and fungicidal substances, and they are used in folk medicine.

Fruits

Avocado
Avocado is a source of vitamin E and vitamin K. Both vitamins may fight some cancer and boost the immune system. It contains monosaturated fat, so it helps lower LDL cholesterol levels. Avocados are a good source of folate and potassium.

Apple
Apples contain antioxidants called flavonoids. This fruit contains vitamins that reduce the risk of cancer. They also help lower the chance of developing diabetes and asthma.

Banana
Bananas are very rich in potassium and may help lower blood pressure levels. They are rich in fibre, potassium, folate and vitamins.

Blackberry
Blackberries get their deep purple colour from the powerful antioxidant anthocyanin. A study shows that the extract may stop the growth of lung cancer cells and may reduce the risk of stroke. It could also treat gout-related symptoms.

Blueberry

Blueberries are near the top when it comes to the antioxidant component. They contain anthocyanins, antioxidant pigment and various phytochemicals. Similar to berry fruits and cranberries, you might want to include them in your daily diet intake, which may help lower the risk of developing age-related diseases such as Parkinson's and Alzheimer's. They also help fight some cancers and inflammation in vitro.

Cantaloupe

Cantaloupe are high in antioxidants and beta carotene, and they help reduce cataracts. Be sure to wash the skin before cutting, because bacteria can grow outside the rind.

Cherry

Rich in the antioxidant anthocyanin, cherries help ease the pain of arthritis and gout.

Cranberry

Cranberries are rich in antioxidants, and they are antibacterial, helping to prevent urinary tract infection.

Fig (Dried)

Figs are a good source of fibre, potassium, calcium and iron. With this content, it reduces the risk of heart disease. Pureed fig is an excellent substitute for fat like butter or oil. In baked goods, simply puree 1 cup (250 ml) dried figs with 1/4 cup (50 ml) water instead of oil, butter or margarine in the recipe.

Grapefruit (Pink)
Pink grapefruit contains lycopene and flavonoids, which protect from some types of cancer. They have soluble fibre that may help lower cholesterol.

Grape
Grapes are rich in antioxidants, and they're rich in resveratrol, which helps prevent heart disease.

Orange
Oranges are a good source of vitamin C, folate and potassium. They contain an important vitamin for pregnant women that helps prevent neural tube defects in their infants. A phytochemical in the fruit lowers triglyceride and blood cholesterol levels. The edible white part of orange rind has nearly the same amount of vitamin C as the flesh, so you might as well eat it, too.

Papaya
Papayas regulate the immune system, help fight infections and are a good source of vitamin C.

Peach
Aside from antioxidant content, the peach is also rich in vitamin C and B-carotene (which is a pro-vitamin that converts into vitamin A in the body, essential for vision).

Pear
Soluble fibre found in this fruit helps prevent constipation, reduce blood cholesterol level and prevent heart disease.

Pineapple

Pineapple contains a natural enzyme called bromelain, which breaks down protein and helps digestion. Bromelain may also prevent blood clots, fight cancer cells and heal wounds faster.

Plum

Plums are low in calories and have no saturated fats. They are an excellent source of vitamin C, dietary fibre and sorbitol.

Tomato

Tomatoes are a good source of vitamin A, folate and potassium. They're the best in lycopene, a potent antioxidant that helps reduce cholesterol levels and protect against advanced-stage prostate cancer.

When tomatoes are cooked with a touch of oil, it provides more lycopene than raw tomatoes.

Raspberry

Raspberries are another antioxidant and help prevent cervical cancer. A research team from Clemson University (CU) Department of Nursing in South Carolina believes that they also help treat esophageal and colon cancer. They are also a source of folate and magnesium.

Strawberry

This fruit is rich in several antioxidants that have anti-inflammatory properties and prevent atherosclerosis (hardened arteries). Strawberries also suppress the progression of cancerous tumours.

Milk and Alternatives

Choose yogurt with 2 percent milk fat (MF) or less. Check food labels because some varieties are higher in calories and sugar.

Choose cheese that has reduced fat or lower fat. Generally some fat cheeses have less than 20 percent milk fat.

Limit cream cheese, ice cream, coffee cream, whipping cream and sour cream because they are high in fat and calories.

Choosing reduced fat content in cheeses does not decrease calcium content—instead, they have a little more calcium.

Meat and Alternatives

Choose an amount up to the size of the palm of your hand and the thickness of your little finger. Choose lean meat, poultry, fish and beans.

Meats
This section includes beef, pork, veal, lamb and game meats such as moose, caribou and deer. Lean and extra lean cuts of meat include inside round roast, outside round roast, eye of round steak, strip loin steak, sirloin steak, rump roast and lean and extra lean ground meat or poultry.

Processed luncheon meat, sausages and prepacked meals are high in sodium and fat. If available, choose low sodium and low fat. You may want to limit intake of this food.

It has been revealed that those who enjoy hamburger, steak and bacon well done were almost five times more likely to develop breast cancer rather than eating rare or medium; this is because of the saturated fats, or the way its prepared. Cooking by grilling, broiling and frying meat at high temperature creates a chemical called heterocychic amines (HCA), which are not present in uncooked meats. HCA are formed when amino acids and creatine (a natural compound found in meat or fish) react at high temperature. Researchers have identified 20 different heterocyclic amines formed during cooking meat that are cancer risks. Eating too much of red meat, fresh or processed, also increases the likelihood of colorectal cancer.

Fish
Fish is a significant source of vitamin D and contributes valuable minerals and nutrients to the diet, such as selenium, iodine, magnesium, iron and copper. Eat at least two food guide servings of fish each week, but do not eat one certain type of fish frequently. You should eat different kinds of fish to reduce the intake of mercury that is present in certain types of fish.

Here are some types of fish and shellfish that contain high levels of fatty acids and are also low in mercury: anchovy, capelin, char, hake, herring, Atlantic mackerel, mullet, pollock (Boston bluefish), salmon, smelt, rainbow trout, lake whitefish, blue crab, shrimp, clam, mussel and oyster.

The types of fish that should be eaten less are fresh or frozen tuna, shark, swordfish, marlin, orange roughy and escolar. If you like to consume these kinds of fish, you should limit your intake. Here is an intake estimate.

- General population: 150 g per week

- Specified women (expectant mothers): 150 g per month

- Children ages 5–11: 125 g per month

- Children ages 1–4: 75 g per month

For reference, 150 grams is 2 food guide servings, or approximately 1 cup.

Canned White Albacore Tuna

(Note that the information below does not apply to canned light tuna.)

- Specified women: 300 g per week (4 food guide servings)

- Children ages 5–11: 150 g per week

- Children ages 1–4: 75 g per week

A reminder that 1 food guide serving is equal to 75 g, 2.5 oz, 125 ml or 1/2 cup. It's also equal to about half of an average can (170 g).

When ordering fish for dining, choose grilled, baked, broiled or poached, and seasoned with herbs and lemon—rather than breaded or fried and with rich sauce.

Canada's Food Guide recommends people eat at least two food guide servings of fish each week.

Meat Alternatives

Eat meat alternatives such as beans, lentils and tofu more often. They are an inexpensive source of protein, are high in fibre and are low in fat.

Use peas, beans and lentils several times a week. Add them to your soup, casseroles, salads and burritos, or mash them into dips.

Choose nuts, nut butter and seeds in small amounts. One food guide serving is 1/4 cup (60 ml) for nuts and seeds, or 2 tablespoons (15 ml) for nut butter.

Fats and Oils

Limit fat to an amount the size of the tip of your thumb. All oils are 100 percent fat, and that means they all have 9 calories per gram. When the label says light, it denotes the flavour and not the calories.

There are different types of fats in foods, including saturated, unsaturated and trans fat. The right amount intake and type of oil and fat can lower the risk of developing certain diseases, such as heart disease. Include a small amount of unsaturated fat, but limit saturated and trans fat in your daily diet.

A small amount is 2–3 tablespoons (30–45 ml) of unsaturated fat for daily intake. This amount includes oil used for cooking, salad dressing, margarine and mayonnaise.

Unsaturated Vegetable Oils: canola, corn, flaxseed, olive, peanut, soybean and sunflower.

The oils considered healthy are olive, sunflower,

flaxseed, walnut and peanut. But even if these oils are known to be healthy, they become unhealthy when they are heated past a certain temperature. You may want to use canola, sunflower or peanut oil for high-temperature cooking.

Limit your intake of butter, hard margarine, lard and shortening.

Here is what a daily intake of unsaturated fat looks like.

Breakfast:
- 1 teaspoon (5 ml) of soft, nonhydrogenated margarine on your toast or bread

- 1 teaspoon (5 ml) canola oil in your pan to make scrambled eggs

Lunch:
- 1 tablespoon (5 ml) of vinegar and oil salad dressing on your salad

Dinner:
- 1 teaspoon (5 ml) of canola or olive oil used to cook your stir fry

In buying margarine, read the label and choose nonhydrogenated with 2 grams or less of saturated and trans fat combined, for the amount of margarine listed in the nutritional facts table.

You have just freshened your memory with the basic food guide, but listen to your body and have a regular check-up with your family physician. Do not compare yourself to other individuals; everyone has a different size, situation and case.

On June 2, 2011, the *New York Times* published an article that said the easiest and quickest way to remember to get a proper diet in every meal is to visually draw a line on a medium-size plate into three different sections. Fill half of your plate with colourful vegetables, eating at least one dark green and one orange vegetable. One-quarter of the plate will be your meat or protein, and the other quarter will be your carbohydrates. Just as what is pictured on the Diabetes Food Guide to Healthy Eating for vegetables and fruits, always go for the rainbow colours, because every colour will give you different cure and nutrition. A good practice and a costless diet is to drink one or two glasses of water before meals. This routine gives me a good bowel movement. Fruits and vegetables that are easily digestible and drinking water before meals make me full more quickly.

A nutritious, balanced diet and healthy snacks will lead you to reduce many illnesses such as stroke, high blood pressure, diabetes and cancer.

Tips on Food Storage

Dairy Products

	Refrigerator	Freezer
Butter	2–3 weeks	6–9 months
Wrap or cover tightly		
Milk	1–2 weeks	not recommended

Check date code. Most milk and similar products are sold in date-coded cartons that indicate the product's peak freshness. Reseal with cap or wrap tightly. Do not return unused portions to original container.

Cream Cheese, Cheese, Cheese Spread	2–4 weeks	not recommended
Hard Cheese (unopened)	3–4 months	6 months
(opened)	2 months	not recommended
Cottage Cheese	10–15 days	not recommended

Check date code. Keep all cheese tightly packed in moisture-proof wrap.

Cream	7–10 days	2 months
Sour Cream	2 weeks	not recommended
Cream Dips opened	1 week	not recommended

Check date code. Most yogurt, creams and similar products are sold in date-coded cartons that indicate a product's peak freshness. Reseal or cover tightly. Do not return unused portions to original container.

Yogurt	10–14 days	not recommended
Frozen Yogurt	n/a	2 months

Check date code. Keep covered.

Eggs

Uncooked	3–4 weeks	not recommended

Check date code. Store eggs in coldest part of refrigerator and in their original container.

Cooked	1 week	not recommended

Store in covered container.

Leftover Egg Dishes	3–4 days	not recommended

Store in covered container.

Fresh Fruits

Apples	1 month	not recommended

Bananas	2–4 days	not recommended
Peaches, Melons, Pears, Avocados	3–5 days	not recommended
Berries and Cherries	2–3 days	12 months
Apricots	3–5 days	not recommended
Grapes	2–5 days	n/a
Pineapple (uncut)	2–3 days	not recommended
Pineapple (cut)	5–7 days	6–12 months

If storing in refrigerator, do not wash fruit before storing. Store in moisture-resistant bags or containers. Wrap cut fruits. Some fruits darken when refrigerated.

Citrus	1–2 weeks	not recommended

Store uncovered.

Juice	6 days	not recommended

Check date code and reseal in original container. Do not return unused portions to original container.

Frozen Juice	Thawing only	12 months

Check date code. Do not refreeze.

Fish and Shellfish

Fish

Fatty Fish (mackerel trout, salmon)	1–2 days	12 months
Lean Fish (cod, flounder, etc.)	1–2 days	6 months
Frozen or Breaded	n/a	3 months

Keep in original wrapper and store in coldest part of refrigerator. Package in vapour-proof and moisture-proof wrap for freezer. Freeze at 0°F. Thaw in refrigerator or check date code. Freeze in original packaging.

Shellfish

Shrimp (uncooked)	1–2 days	12 months
Crab	3–5 days	10 months
Cooked Fish or Shellfish	2–3 days	3 months

Freeze package in vapour- and moisture-proof container.

Meat

Fresh (uncooked)

Chops	2–3 days	6–12 months
Ground	1 day	3–4 months
Roast	2–4 days	6–12 months
Bacon	1–2 weeks	1–2 months
Sausage	1–2 days	1–2 months
Steak	2–4 days	6–9 months
Poultry	1 day	12 months
Lunch Meat	3–5 days	1 month

Check date code for use. Store in coldest part of refrigerator in original packaging. Use additional moisture- and vapour-proof container for freezing. Recommended refrigerator temperature 33–36°F and freezer temperature 0–2°F.

Cooked

Meat	2–3 days	2–3 months
Poultry	2–3 days	4–5 months
Ham	1–2 weeks	1–2 months

Check date code for use. Store in coldest part of refrigerator in original packaging. Place package in moisture- and vapour-proof container for freezing.

Food Safety Issues

People with cancer need to be especially careful about food safety, because cancer and treatments like chemotherapy can weaken your immune system. Your body may be less able to fight infection from bacteria or other organisms that could be in foods. You should be in a habit of reading labels and ingredients that you buy in groceries, and be particularly picky with produce. Even if you do not have cancer, it is wise to do the same. What you eat is what you become.

Prepare, cook and store your foods with care.

- Wash your hands with warm, soapy water before and after preparing food, and before eating.

- Wash vegetables and fruit thoroughly under running water before peeling or cutting.

- Avoid vegetables and fruit that can't be washed well.

- Scrub vegetables and fruit that have firm surfaces, such as potatoes, carrots, oranges and melons.

- Cut away any damaged or bruised areas on produce; bacteria can thrive in these places.

- Wash the top lids of canned foods with soap and water before opening.

- Rinse packaged salads under running water even when marked "prewashed."

- Refrigerate foods at or below 4°C (40°F).

- Thaw meat, fish or poultry in the microwave or refrigerator (not on the counter).

- Put food in the refrigerator within two hours of serving. Foods containing eggs, cream or mayonnaise should be refrigerated after no more than one hour.

- Use defrosted foods right away and do not refreeze them.

- Cook meats until well done, with no traces of pink in the centre. Red meats should be cooked to an internal temperature of 77°C (170°F), or 71°C (160°F) if the meat is ground. Poultry should be cooked to an internal temperature of 85°C (185°F), or 74°C (165°F) if ground or in pieces (breasts, legs, thighs). A meat thermometer is your only way to be sure of the internal temperature.

- Use different spoons to taste and stir your food while you are cooking it.

- Cool hot foods, uncovered, in the refrigerator. Place in storage containers after cooling. Freeze what you do not plan to use within the next two to three days. Throw out all prepared foods after three days in the refrigerator.

- Throw out entire food packages or containers with any mould, including yogurt, cheese, cottage cheese, fruit, vegetables, jelly, and bread and pastry products.

- Keep work surfaces and kitchen equipment clean.

- Use separate cutting boards for raw foods and cooked foods. Use one cutting board for fresh produce and a different one for raw meat, poultry and seafood.

- Wash cutting boards after each use in hot, soapy water or in the dishwasher.

- Get rid of worn cutting boards.

- Keep appliances, countertops and kitchen surfaces free of food crumbs.

- Consider using paper towels to wipe kitchen surfaces, or change dishcloths daily to avoid the possibility of cross-contamination and the spread of bacteria.

- Wash dishcloths in the hot cycle of the washing machine.

- Avoid using sponges because they are harder to keep bacteria-free.

- Clean and sanitize countertops, cutting boards and utensils each week with a disinfectant cleaner or a mild bleach solution of 5 ml (1 teaspoon) of bleach per 750 ml (3 cups) of water.

Vitamin, Mineral and Herbal Supplements
The best way to obtain vitamins, minerals or other nutrients is by eating healthy foods. Cancer and its treatments may make it difficult to eat healthily for an extended period of time, so a daily vitamin and mineral supplement may be recommended. Talk to your doctor to see if vitamin and mineral supplements are appropriate and safe to use, especially if you are having chemotherapy or radiation therapy.

Some people consider using nutritional supplements or natural health products. "Natural" does not always mean safe. These products may also interfere with other medications or treatments. Always talk to your doctor about nutritional supplements or natural health products before taking them.

Testimonials

Like me, maybe your friends and family have told you what they hear, read and see on the Internet or TV regarding different kinds of food and herbs, and ways to get well. There is so much information that you cannot conform to it all. A little research will help you decide what to do or not to do. Above all, listen to your body.

Even if you are eating healthy foods, you may experience the following: irritable bowel syndrome, migraines, indigestion, heartburn, joint pain, eczema, bloating, stomach pain, sleeplessness and weight gain. These can all be symptoms of food intolerance. Food intolerance is by trial and error, going on an elimination diet for a few weeks and observing the results. Symptoms are not always related, and we consume different foods, so this diet is hard to track. If you are diagnosed with a sensitivity to yeast, healthy fruits like grapes and blueberries should be avoided because the skins of these fruits contain yeast. In this case you may want to have a blood test for food intolerance.

Canada Cancer Society research has shown that eating a healthy diet can help prevent some cancers from developing in the first place. As far as cancer coming back, some research does suggest that eating a healthy diet may prevent cancer from returning. Research has also shown that obesity increases the risk of some cancers returning, so maintaining a healthy body weight is important.

If you are living with advanced cancer, you will have different challenges in eating well and maintaining your body weight. Talk to your health-care team about ways to meet your nutritional needs. Eating a healthy diet as much as possible will help you feel better, keep up your strength and help you cope with side effects such as fatigue and loss of appetite.

A very important nutrient-giving food that I read about on a healthy magazine is the flax seed. It is a tiny seed but is a gigantic help. It is high in most of the B vitamins, magnesium and manganese. This seed is rich in omega-3 fatty acids, which are a key force against inflammation in our bodies. Inflammation plays a part of many chronic diseases, including heart disease, arthritis, asthma, diabetes and some cancers. This inflammation is enhanced by having too little omega-3 intake, which you get from fish, flax and walnuts. The seed is also good for preventing Alzheimer's disease, and it helps increase memory.

Every morning I prepare a fruit smoothie breakfast not just for myself but for the whole family. I blend different fruits in the morning and puree with two tablespoons of flax seed. My kids enjoy the different fruits every day. I also mix flax seed in spaghetti sauce, casseroles and pancakes.

Flax seed has a great percentage of fibre, and it is a perfect aid to lose weight. I used to have bowel movement problems that worried me so much that I had to buy fibre powder mixed with water to drink every day, to regulate it. After I heard about the health benefits of blueberries, I now add this fruit to my daily diet. I see to it that I have at least one cup of blueberries every day. I snack on the fruit itself, or I eat it as my breakfast and pour milk and mix with one teaspoon flax seed. I feel the difference, my bowel movement is regulated and I don't need the fibre drink anymore. This inexpensive fruit, which I buy either fresh or frozen, is good for anyone. First of all, blueberries are high in vitamin C, a strong antioxidant offering support for the immune system. Blueberries also contain fibre, folate, iron, manganese, potassium, calcium, magnesium, phosphorus, sodium, zinc, copper, B vitamins, vitamin E and silicon. All that in a little berry!

Blueberries have been getting so much attention in the news lately because the ongoing research on phytochemicals reveals blueberries atop the list in antioxidant-rich foods. Blueberries contain a huge list of phytochemicals: phenolic acid, anthocyanins (the pigment that makes them blue), ellagic acid (which may inhibit tumour growth), alpha carontene, beta carotene (precursor to vitamin A), caryophyllene (possible anti-inflammatory), photogenic acid, eugenol, limonene, thymol (antiseptic and antifungal properties), catechins, tocopherols and tocotrienols (vitamin E family).

Eating healthy will boost your overall personality, giving you more energy and vitality, and you will feel good inside and out.

Activities

An increase in physical activity in your daily life will definitely be a lifesaver. You may consult your doctor before you start any vigorous activities, but for a start, you could just have a moderate exercise like walking or biking. A treadmill is a great help, but when your body gets used to exercise, you may want to do a variety of exercises to build muscle in the places where you want it to be, tone the whole body and have good posture.

I see to it that I have at least three hours of exercise in a week. I found a challenging workout video with Chris Freytag, which my sister gave to me. The workout burns fat, flattens abs and tones my whole body. The moves never bore me because of different circuit intervals that consist of cardio moves, strength training and abdomen exercises. Check it out at www.goodtimes.com.

Rest

This is an important part of our lives. A power nap during the day and a quality sleep is helpful. As a rule of thumb we should sleep seven to eight hours per day. If we sleep six hours or fewer, we are at risk of an accident. Research by Michael H. Bonnet, PhD, and Donna L. Arand Dayton at the Veterans Affairs Medical Center show that those who sleep more than nine hours per day do not live as long as their eight-hour counterparts. Too much and too little sleep puts you at risk.

A nap for at least fifteen minutes is powerful. You can make yourself more alert and patient, reduce stress, increase learning, be more efficient and have better health,according to Elizabeth Scott, MS, on her stress management article.

Visit Your Doctor Regularly after Treatment Care

Take notes in a diary to track your daily routine and things to ask the doctors the next time you see them. This habit is an important task.

Name Telephone Purpose of Visit How Often to Visit

Family Doctor

Oncology Doctor

Surgeon

Other Specialists

Notes:_____

_____

_____

_____

_____

When should I call my
oncologist?_____

When should I call my family doctor? _____

_____

When should I call other doctors or care providers
involved in my care?

_____

Advice from your Care Team

_____

_____

Screening tests (to check for
cancer)_____

Eating habits (especially if you are diabetic)_____

_____

_____

_____

_____

Exercise (consult your doctor, especially if you have hypertension)

_____

_____

_____

_____

_____

Healthy weight programs

_____

_____

_____

_____

Sunscreen

_____

_____

Immunizations

_____

_____

_____

Help to quit smoking and tobacco

_____

_____

_____

Support groups

_____

_____

_____

Counselling (individual, couples, family)

_____

_____

_____

Sleep

_____

_____

_____

Complementary and alternative medicine

_____

_____

_____

Preventing osteoporosis (weak bones)

_____

_____

_____

Other

_____

_____

_____

Below is a list of topics that can concern you after the treatment.

Topic	My Concern	Person Who Can Help
My relationships		
Legal issues		
Spiritual issues		
Money problems		
My job		
My rights at work		
Financial planning		
Estate planning		
Long-term care		
Health insurance		
Life insurance		
Nutrition		

Emotional support		
Health changes		
Fear of cancer return (recurrence)		
Other		

Some people work their hearts out to make and save money ... but in the long run they lose their money to save their health. I have designed HUG KISS to become financially healthy.

HOW U GET TO KNOW
IMPORTANT, SIMPLE STEPS

(HUG KISS)

To become financially healthy:

Diagnose your financial standing:

- What you own

- Wills

Identify your goals and objectives:

- Reducing or eliminating debts

- Providing education fund

- Providing for early retirement

Identify problems, analyze your situation and create steps to achieve your desired results:

- Are you financially ready?

- Alternative solutions

- Mystery of protection

- Do it now.

- Perform periodic reviews and updates.

Diagnose Your Financial Standing

a) Gather the Facts, Which Include What You Own
Current and potential assets and liabilities

Once people start to earn a living, they can't find time to do this simple thing: make an inventory of current and potential assets and liabilities. Jotting a list of all your possessions is important while you are alive, and even after your death. You may want to do this step as a part of your effort to organize your life.

Assets are things that you own; they could be liquid assets and tangible assets

Liquid assets: cash on hand, monthly income from all sources, money in bank, investments, life insurance, accounts receivable and anything that could easily be disposed of. Make a file to keep recent bank account statements, investments from mutual companies or insurance companies, employment profit shares certificate and insurance policies.

Tangible assets: real estate, cars, jewelry, paintings and furniture and household contents. Walk through your house and take pictures at different angles of your valuables.

Listing your assets is useful in determining the value of your estate. First and foremost, you could easily find how much coverage you need for fire and theft insurance. And if you lost some content or belongings due to fire and theft, your list becomes handy to assess the amount of losses incurred in case of a claim.

Liabilities are an inevitable part of our lives, so have a list of what you owe, just like what you have done with your assets: mortgage, car loans, other personal loans, loans from your insurance policies, credit cards, income tax arrears and property taxes.

You have just identified your assets and liabilities. Total all your assets minus your total liabilities, and the answer is what you own.

b) Make a Will

As soon as you make an inventory of your assets and liabilities, make a will, especially if you have dependents. No matter how much we own, it is important to have a will and make it current. We don't know where life will take us; even if at the present you have a perfect health, you can't go wrong in writing a will. If you don't have a will, your family will have a hard time financially and will spend more money and time to fight for what they should have received. Also, if you are living in a common-law relationship, a will is the only way your common-law spouse may inherit your property in the event of your death.

For example, Jason was married to Nancy for years. During that period he made a will and named Nancy as his executor and the sole beneficiary. When their relationship soured, Jason left Nancy without divorcing her. They also didn't file any legal separation.

A few years later, Jason met Patty, and they started a family. Jason didn't rewrite the will because he thought he was in perfect health, and he did not want to take the time to amend it. Patty did not know about the will. Two years later, Jason had a massive headache and was admitted to the hospital, where he died. In this case, Nancy inherited all of his assets in accordance with the will.

A will is a written instrument that conveys a person's intentions about how assets should be distributed after his or her death. Because every person has a different life situation, a will is not a "one size fits all" document. Although you can find a prepared template for a will in a book or online, it might not be suited to your specific case. It is always wise to get the advice of a legal professional when you are considering the terms of your will. A paralegal may be able to help you and will likely cost less than a traditional lawyer. However, if you have a complex situation, it might be best to speak with a lawyer. Make some phone calls or ask some friends if they can recommend a qualified lawyer who can provide the assistance you need at a reasonable cost.

In the past, wills were the only formal document that could be used for estate planning. Today, our lives are often more complicated, and there are different documents and agreements that can be used as part of an estate plan to be carried out with informed advice from financial, legal and tax professionals.

In Ontario there are two types of wills that are valid. The holographic will is a hard copy with the signature of the testator. A legal will is also written instruction by the testator, but he signed it in front of two witnesses and a legal counsellor.

As mentioned earlier, be sure to have a complete list of

what you wanted to include in the will. Meet with your financial advisor for support on advanced concepts such as case consultation, large case illustration, tax and estate planning, actuarial and underwriting before meeting with a legal advisor; this will save you time and cost.

You and your spouse should know and understand the provisions written in each individual will. Some people think that if you die without a will, all your assets will be awarded to the government. That is not true; the government is the last beneficiary, only if you do not have any traceable next of kin. In Ontario, if you die without a will, this is how your property would be divided according to provincial legislation regulating the division of family assets, marriage contracts and supplemental pension plans.

- If you have a spouse with no children, all your assets will go to your spouse.

- If you have one or more children without a spouse, all your assets will be distributed equally to all of your children.

- If you have a spouse and one child, the first $75,000 goes to the spouse and the remainder is split equally.

- If you have a spouse and multiple children, the first $75,000 goes to your spouse, one-third of the remainder goes to spouse and two-thirds of remainder go to the children.

- If you do not have a spouse or children, all of your assets goes to your closest next of kin, usually in the following order: parents; if neither is alive then brothers or sisters; if none are alive then nephews or nieces; if none are alive then next of kin. If there is no traceable next of kin, all assets are turned over to the government.

A spouse means a husband or wife. It excludes common-law spouses in most cases.

Choose the Executor of Your Estate

In making a will, appoint someone to have a legal authority to carry out what would you wish to be done. This appointed person in your will is called the estate executor. Your executor could be a member of your family, a close friend or someone who could handle an estate, like a trust company. It is preferable to appoint a person who at least has experience in finance, business and law, and a person who has a lot of patience and time. Above all, he or she should be willing to be an executor.

Here are some important duties of an executor: find the original will, advise family and friends, assist in paying funeral expenses, identify deceased's creditors, pay income tax, tackle daily tasks like redirect mail, handle outstanding bills and execute the provisions of the will. Usually the spouse is named estate executor and trustee. Depending on your situation, you may want to hire a lawyer as your executor; he could be paid a certain percentage of your assets, be paid by the hour or have a flat fee.

If the spouse is not the sole beneficiary, it's a good idea to also name a relative, friend or colleague in whom you have complete trust, or to call upon the services of a specialist such as a notary, lawyer or trust company. Even if your spouse is the sole beneficiary, one of these persons should also be designated as a substitute, just in case your spouse predeceases you or is unable to perform his or her duties as estate executor.

Probating a Will
Probate is the process of getting the court to declare a will is legally valid before an executor executes his or her task. Not all wills have to go through this process.

Identify Your Goals and Objectives

Set goals that are short-term or long-term and that are achievable in a given range of time. If you don't have any vision as to what you want to become and where you want to be, it is just like walking on a grey cloud with no hope and happiness, or living today and failing tomorrow.

There are many possible stages of life: when you are single, married, married with children, divorced or separated, becoming old. Every stage of life has a different aim, so plan ahead of time by identifying your goals and objectives, which include:

- paying oneself first by putting aside at least 10 percent of your income to start saving

- reducing or eliminating debts

It is time to review your long-term and short-term loans.

Mortgages. Get your current statement of mortgage checked, if it is about to renew and get your latest balance. You might consider renewing from another lender to take advantage of a low interest rate. Low interest rates are always good, but be cautious when transferring to another lender. Check all those fine lines on your current lender's agreement regarding penalties in case you break a contract, and determine if it is worth it to do so. You may want to talk to a broker about shopping around on interest rates, because a broker could run your credit record once, and he could access different lenders. If you shop by yourself, every lender you approach will run your credit history, and by doing that, it lowers your beacon score.

Credit Cards. Do not collect credit cards from every store that offers you one. Keep one or a maximum of two, and choose cards with the lowest interest rates even if they charge an annual fee if you carry a balance. There are some rewards, points and added features on credit cards that charge a certain fee or that charge high interest rates; these cards are good to have only if you do not carry a balance. You may want to ask the credit card issuers to lessen the interest rate they charge you, if you think you are being charged more than other card issuers and you are good at managing your payment due dates.

Lines of Credit
Unsecured Line of Credit

This is an easy access of cash, and less paperwork is required from you because there is no collateral. This is fully based on one's credit beacon score. The beacon score is determined by using a credit bureau by the lender to see your credit history, and the higher score you have, the healthier credit you have. Since there is nothing to back up this type of loan, it charges higher interest rates than a secured one. You may use this for buying a car, house renovation, education or debt consolidation.

Secured Line of Credit

As the title implies, it means the lender is holding a security base on the equity or value of your house. You could access more money to pay that large home renovation, or you could perform debt consolidation. The processing on this type of loan is longer but offers lower interest rates compared to the unsecured line of credit.

You pay interest every month, without paying any principal. Make use of your line of credit to pay off your high-interest credit card. Managing your debt is one way to reach a healthy living.

Providing an Education Fund
In Canada and particularly in Ontario, there is a Canada Education Savings Grant (CESG), which means the government will match your contributions by 20 percent up to $400 per year, and an additional CESG will be given once qualified. The lifetime limit for the fund per child is $50,000. In addition, the CESG program is eligible to get a $500 Canada Learning Bond (CLB). The CLB is a grant that helps you start saving for your child's postsecondary education. The government of Canada will make a payment of $500 directly into your child's Registered Education Savings Plan (RESP). In order to get the CLB, you have to open an RESP for your child through your insurance advisor, scholarship trust foundation, credit union or bank. The government will deposit $500 into your child's RESP and could provide an extra $100 per year based on eligibility, for up to

15 years. Each child could get up to $2,000 to spend toward education after high school.

Most educational funds offer life insurance when you start the fund; if something happens to you or your spouse, the future contributions will be waived.

Building a Start-Up Fund for a Business
If you are an entrepreneur and decide to create your own business, you have to set a reachable goal. You will set up a business to generate money, but you have to have capital to begin with. You should have the expertise and knowledge regarding what business you are going into. Plan all your financial resources available—like taking out equity on your property, savings or investment or whether taking out a loan from a financial institution, from relatives or friends—and draw a map. You have to spend modestly. Businesses fail because of many factors: lack of funds, overspending and lack of expertise and knowledge.

Providing for Early Retirement

This information is important in determining the best strategy to be used to help you attain your goals. The younger age you start saving for your retirement, the more time you have to generate more funds.

The government constantly proposes changes on pension plans. The Canada Pension Plan might not sustain its obligations, and Old Age Security benefits will be reduced. With our economy today, there is less job security in the province. While you can, take advantage on accounts that save on taxes and accumulate savings.

The government is encouraging everyone to prepare for their retirement by contributing to Tax Free Savings Account (TFSA), Registered Retirement Savings Plan (RRSP) and Registered Retirement Income Fund (RRIF).

Tax Free Savings Account (TFSA)

This type of savings was launched in 2009 to individuals age 18 or older with a Social Security Number (SIN) to assist them to accumulate savings and its earnings, without paying taxes on them; even the withdrawals made are tax-free.

The Canada Revenue Ruling on TFSA is that each qualified individual may contribute up to a maximum of $5,000 per year. If you were not able to contribute the maximum, you may carry over that balance to the following year. For example:

2011 contribution room for Jason is $5,000
2011 Jason contributed $3,500
2011 unused contribution $1,500

2012 contribution room for Jason is $5,000
2011 unused amount $1,500
2012 total contribution allowed is $6,500

When a withdrawal was made, the total amount withdrawn is added to the next year. For example:

2011 contribution room for Gianne is $5,000
2011 Gianne contributed $4,000
2011 unused contribution $1,000
2011 Gianne withdraw $2,000

2012 contribution room for Gianne $5,000
Add unused contribution in 2011 $1,000

Add withdrawal made in 2011 $2,000
Total contribution allowed In 2012 $8,000

Once you overcontribute on your TFSA, you will be charged a penalty of 1 percent on the excess TFSA of each month that an excess exists in the account. For example:

2010 contribution room for Krizia is $5,000
2010 on March 8 she contributed $3,000
2010 on August 20 she contributed $4,000
Her total contribution in 2010 $7,000
Excess on the contribution is $2,000

If she didn't realize till December that she overcontributed her TFSA, this is the penalty calculation:

Excess exist on the account $2,000
1% penalty $20
from August to December 5 months
$2,000 × 1% × 5 months
Total amount payable $100

In spite of the simple ruling imposed on TFSA clients, the rule seems to be misunderstood quite a bit. The Canada Revenue Agency notified approximately 70,000 TFSA clients this year for a probability of overcontribution on their TFSA last year, and those people tend to pay more taxes.

A clear understanding will better serve your purpose.

Registered Retirement Savings Plan (RRSP)

Any person who has an employment income could contribute to the RRSP up to the age of 71. You may contribute up to 18 percent of earned income from the prior year, or the maximum amount limit allowed. Pension adjustment (PA), past service pension adjustment (PSPA), pension adjustment reversals (Revs) and unused RRSP deduction limit room at the end of the previous year are also used to calculate the limit.

Maximum Limits

2011 $22,450
2012 $22,970
2013 $23,820

RRSP has unique features such as the following:

- Income tax deductible

- Deferred income tax on investment income (i.e., interest income, dividend income, capital gains)

- Ability to pay by preauthorized cheque

- Amount withdrawn being included as your income and being taxed accordingly

You may open an RRSP to any financial institution or life insurance company. Segregated funds offered by the insurance companies differ from that of a mutual fund.

Segregated Funds versus Mutual Funds

Segregated Funds

- The funds are protected against financial turbulence and capital invested up to 100 percent.

- Creditors proofed.

- Death benefit: If beneficiaries are named by the owner, upon death the probate tax or fee is waived.

A mutual fund does not offer the above-mentioned features that a segregated fund has, but the probate fee might also be waived if the beneficiary has been named in mutual funds.

Every insurance company offers different investment funds and different fund managers. There are several types of savings options with many features to help you achieve your savings goal.

Daily Interest Fund. This kind of savings accumulates interest and funds to make an investment on a daily basis.

Guaranteed Investment Fund. This is an option for stable return and capital protection.

Investment Fund. A wealth-building potential similar to that of a mutual fund. Fund managers invest in stocks, bonds or other assets; you may select from low-risk to high-risk portfolios, depending on your fund's investment objectives. It also offers valuable wealth-protection features.

Registered Retirement Income Fund (RRIF). RRSP should be transferred to RRIF or another pension plan before you turn 71. Canada Revenue will register the total RRSP amount you accumulated over the years to a carrier to which it is being transferred. No contributions are allowed once done. The carrier will allow you to withdraw gradually, and you pay taxes only on the portion withdrawn annually. There is no maximum amount for the withdrawals.

Identifying Problems

Life is full of ifs. If health goes wrong, you ask, "Am I financially prepared?"

Life is uncertain, but only three things are going to happen to every one of us: either we die too soon or we live too long; once we reach an old age, we get sick along the way, and long-term care is needed; and life will be easier if we are financially prepared. Each situation will be a challenge. No one can prevent these things from happening but you can prepare when it happens.

The Three Uncertainties

1. *If you die too soon*

   Your death will be a burden to your loved ones if you are not financially prepared.

2. *If you live too long*

   You will outlive your savings and investments. If you are financially prepared, you will continue to enjoy your life fully.

3. *Growing old*

   Along the way, more uncertainties happen. For example, you get sick, and it could be mild, critical or terminal, or you become disabled. When you get to the point that you lose independence, you are a burden to your family. A loss of independence is the inability to perform two of the following activities of daily living without the help of another person:

- Bathing

- Dressing

- Toileting

- Transferring

- Eating

- Continence

Or a loss of independence is a cognitive impairment that endangers your health or safety (e.g., Alzheimer's).

Facts Regarding Age 65
Group Insurance

Many benefits plans and most long-term disability contracts terminate at age 65. However, most provincial health plans pay for most drug costs over 65.

Canada Pension Plan (CPP)

Workers receive CPP at age 65 and will continue to work as usual. You may choose to receive your CPP earlier at age 60 while working, but you may do so at a reduced rate. Once you start receiving CPP, you can no longer contribute to CPP.

Survivor Benefits for Age 65 and Older

At age 65 and older, the benefit is equal to 60 percent of the retirement pension payable to the deceased survivor. If the survivor is 65 and is receiving a retirement pension, the benefit is combined with the retirement pension.

Old Age Supplement (OAS)

You are entitled to receive OAS at age 65 even if you continue to earn an income. However, you will receive less OAS if your income exceeds $56,968 based on the 2002 rate, and OAS ends if your net income is above $92,381.

RRSP/RRIF

The new rule set by the federal government in 2007 is that a person can draw pension at age 71, and an individual can contribute until age 71. Seniors are now encouraged to work or continue to be employed while they can, until the age 71.

Things will be better with preparation. You should write that living will and power of attorney.

Living Will

A living will is an instruction written by you that serves as a guideline when you suffer with terminal illness, or a helpless condition. It is a practical way to fulfil one's wishes and to ensure a gentle and natural death.

In this modern society, there is so much amazing technology and advanced medical research. Scientists have the ability to create new medicines and can use different tactics to keep people alive. While waiting for further prognosis, you might want to leave an instruction in writing for the following reasons. When you are still capable of talking and thinking, you could still decide to continue or discontinue your medical treatment, but if you cannot express what you want, the doctor has to discuss it with the immediate family and nursing personnel; it is up to the discretion of the doctors to continue or discontinue the treatment. In this respect, they will follow your instructions.

If you fear being kept alive by artificial means, only to suffer and die anyway, let them know in writing. If you reach a point when you think that prescribed treatment is no longer useful or effective, you might want to refuse further treatments.

A living will is not a law that everyone should follow, and it can't force doctors and hospitals to follow what was written, but it is a guideline and a subtle way of reassuring the family. It serves as a guide for the doctor, who has the ultimate decision with respect for what you want to happen. A living will need to be reviewed and revised if necessary, especially if your family situation changes.

Living Will versus Power of Attorney

Living will and power of attorney apply only when you are alive and become invalid upon death. They are almost always mistaken as the same thing.

Living will only addresses your treatment and personal care wishes; it does not need to name anyone or be written in a certain way.

Power of attorney is a legal document that gives authority to someone to act on your behalf; this someone is called your "attorney." Attorney in Canada does not usually mean a lawyer. However, you can write your treatment wishes as part of power of attorney.

Living Will versus Last Will and Testament

Last will and testament applies upon your death. It covers the distribution of your property after you die.

There are three kinds of power of attorney in Ontario.

General Power of Attorney for Property

This type of power of attorney is normally used in business or for short-term, temporary reasons. It is a legal document that authorizes your attorney to manage your finances and property only while you are mentally capable. Once you are mentally incapacitated from managing your property, the general power of attorney for property become useless and the person can no longer act for you.

Continuing Power of Attorney for Property

Power of attorney for property can make a continuing power of attorney for property instead. Continuing power of attorney for property allows your attorney to act for you even you become mentally incapacitated from managing your property. Your attorney has the authority to do so for this purpose only. The document becomes valid as soon as you sign and are witnessed. You may instruct in writing on the same document that it will become effective on a specific date you want. You might need assistance from your lawyer.

You can give a valid continuing power of attorney for property if you are at least 18 years of age and are mentally capable of doing so. Mental capacity in this case means you must:

- know what property you have and its approximate value

- be aware of your obligations to the people who depend on you financially

- know what you are giving your attorney the authority to do

- know that your attorney is required to account for the decisions made about your property

- know that as long as you are mentally capable, you can revoke this power of attorney

- understand that if your attorney does not manage your property well, its value may decrease

- understand that there is always a chance that your attorney could misuse his or her authority

Even if you are incapable of managing your property, you may be capable of giving a continuing power of attorney. For example, you may not remember how much your monthly pension cheque is, but you may know that you get one and that you want your daughter to handle it.

You can appoint anyone to be your attorney who is 18 years or older. It is important to give careful thought to whom you choose. You must consider the following:

1. Whether he or she is trustworthy and good at handling money;

2. Whether he or she is willing to act as your attorney; and

3. Whether he or she expects some payment.

You may appoint more than one attorney, but all your attorneys will have to agree before a decision can be made on your behalf—unless you state in the document that they can make decisions separately. When two or more attorneys must agree on a decision, they are said to act jointly. When you state that they can make decisions together or separately, they are said to act jointly and severally.

In writing your continuing power of attorney for property, you may consider to name a substitute attorney. This person can act for you if your first attorney or attorneys cannot or will not act for you when the time comes.

You need at least two witnesses when you sign the document. The following people cannot be witnesses:

- Your spouse, partner, child or someone you treat as your child

- Your attorney or your attorney's spouse or partner

- Anyone under the age of 18

- Anyone who has a guardian of property appointed for him or her by a court because the person is not mentally capable of managing property

- Anyone who has a guardian of the person appointed for them by a court because he or she is not mentally capable of making his or her own personal care decisions

You could cancel your power of attorney after you have signed. As long as you are mentally capable of making a continuing power of attorney for property, you can take it back, cancel it or revoke it, but you must do so in writing. Two people must witness (the aforementioned witness restrictions apply) when signing this statement that you want to revoke it. There is no special form for this statement, which is referred to as revocation.

Continuing power of attorney for property ends when you die or when your attorney dies, becomes incapable or resigns—unless you named more than one attorney, or you named a substitute. A court appoints a guardian of the person for you when you sign a new continuing power of attorney for property, unless the new one says that you want more than one continuing power of attorney for property, or when you revoke the power of attorney while you are still mentally capable.

If you have not made a continuing power of attorney for property, and you become mentally incapable of managing your property, then one of the following things could happen:

1. Some of your property, such as pensions and social benefits, could be managed informally by friends or relatives.

2. Someone could go to court and ask to be appointed to formally manage your property as your guardian of property.

3. The Office of the Public Guardian and Trustee could be appointed to manage your property. This is called a statutory guardianship. In this case, a close relative can apply to the Public Guardian and Trustee to take over the formal management of your property.

Making a continuing power of attorney for property lets you choose a person you trust to protect your property and your interests, if the need arises.

Power of Attorney for Personal Care

Personal care deals only with personal care decisions.

The law says your doctor and other health-care providers must get your substitute decision maker's consent before taking action, if you become mentally incapable of making personal care decisions. Your substitute decision maker (SDM) will decide for you.

Making this document lets you choose a person you trust to be your substitute decision maker if you become mentally incapable in the future. This is also a way to make sure your wishes about personal care decisions will be respected. It gives you a chance to say what you want and do not want. For example, if you do not want certain medical treatments if you get seriously ill, then you can state this in your power of attorney.

This document takes effect only if you become mentally incapable of making some or all of your personal care decisions. On the other hand, a continuing power of attorney for property comes into effect as soon as it is signed and witnessed, unless you state otherwise. Power of attorney documents are often kept in a safe place, to use only in the event of mental incapacity at a later date.

Depending on the situation, you are mentally incapacitated of personal care decision if your attorney would decide this, unless you name someone else in your power of attorney to confirm that you are mentally incapable. If you do name someone else, your attorney cannot start making personal care decisions for you until that other person confirms that you are incapable of making decisions. If your attorney thinks you might be mentally incapable, he or she must arrange for that person to assess you and confirm your incapacity.

You can name certain individual—such as your family

doctor, another health professional or even a personal friend—to confirm that you are mentally incapable. You could also state that you would like your mental incapacity confirmed without naming an individual or profession; if you do this, it will be confirmed by a capacity assessor, which is someone trained and approved to determine mental incapacity. Sometimes, anyone else (other than your attorney or whoever you named) could decide that you are mentally incapable of making personal care decisions when you are in situations concerning your health treatment, admission to a long-term care facility or the need for personal assistance services such as bathing and eating while you are in a long-term care facility. However, if this happens you have the right to have the decision reviewed by the Provincial Consent and Capacity Board. The Consent and Capacity Board is an independent body that holds hearing to consider a variety of things, including a review of an individual's capacity to make decisions about health treatment, personal assistance services or admission to a long-term care facility. The appointment of a representative lets one make treatment decisions for someone who is incapable of making decisions and a substitute decision maker's request for guidance in making treatment decisions.

Health practitioners (i.e., doctors, nurses, dentists, physiotherapists, occupational therapists, psychologists and psychiatrists) cannot treat you without your consent. If they decide that you are incapable of making decisions about your treatment, then they must get the consent of your substitute decision maker. This means your attorney or other substitute decision maker cannot make treatment decisions for you unless a health practitioner first decides that you are incapable of making them yourself.

Only an evaluator decides whether you are capable of making your own decisions about entering a long-term care facility. An evaluator must be a nurse, doctor, psychologist, psychiatrist, occupational therapist, social worker, physiotherapist, speech language therapist or audiologist.

Your attorney cannot make these decisions for you unless an evaluator finds that you are incapable of making them yourself. Your attorney could make a decision if you become mentally incapable. If you give instructions or express wishes about your personal care while you are capable, your attorney must follow them if you become incapable.

You cannot name as your attorney someone who is paid to give you health care or residential, social, support or training services (unless this person is your spouse, partner or relative).

Why Hinder?

Most people don't like buying insurance, and neither do they enjoy writing their will or a cohabitation agreement. They think, "Why worry about things that could go wrong when everything is going so well?" The same goes with assigning someone power of attorney for property and personal care. Losing one's physical and mental capacities is a very disturbing thought. Nevertheless, it happens to others every day, and it could also happen to you at any time. If, following an illness or accident, you were to become unable to take care of yourself or administer your property, who would do it for you? And more important, how would it be done? The power of attorney for property and personal care answers these and other questions, should such an event occur.

Planning One's Funeral

No matter the circumstances, a death in the family is always a difficult ordeal. Many people now make their own funeral arrangements in order to relieve loved ones of this heart-wrenching burden. If such is the case, your family should be informed of what has been prearranged (burial, cremation, final resting place, etc.). Reputable funeral homes can also be asked to take care of all the details and inform you of the costs.

Donating Your Organs

More and more people are donating one or several organs, and even their bodies to science. Today, it's easy to donate your eyes, kidneys or other organs. In some provinces, all you need to do is check a box on your driver's license. Inform your family of your decision to donate organs when you die. It's preferable to carry your organ donor authorization card with you at all times, in case of accidental death.

Organize your documents. You should indicate the nature of all your important documents and be sure to store them in a secured place, like a safety deposit box at a banking institution. It is wise to make several copies, keep one in your personal file and give one to your legal advisor. We are now in the world of high technology, and most baby boomers want to store a soft copy, but it will be hard for your family to retrieve them, so you might stick to hard copies.

Be reminded that a safety deposit box can no longer

be kept under seal in the event of a person's death, ever since the succession of taxes were abolished. Estate executors are now being allowed access to the deceased's safety deposit box upon proof of his or her designation as such, which is usually established by probating the will and presenting the owner's death certificate. Since a delay of about a month will be inevitable as part of probate, some documents should not be stored in a safety deposit box at the banking institutions, like insurance policies and wills. Beneficiaries should have immediate access and should submit a claim, which is practical to do.

In regard to wills, a lawyer may keep the original as the person who drew it up, or you may keep it with the trust company that has been designated as the executor of the estate. Commercial partnership agreements should also be kept in a safe place.

The following documents are vital to your family in case of death and total disability.

- Personal information (includes immediate family and next of kin, with their contact numbers)
- Your will
- Funeral arrangements
- Birth certificate
- Citizenship papers
- Marriage contract or certificate
- Cohabitation agreement
- Residence and properties

- Registered Retirement Savings Plans
- Locked-in retirement account
- Bank accounts
- Securities and investments
- Debtors and creditors
- Clubs and associations
- Income tax returns
- Other assets
- Your accountant
- Life insurance agent
- General insurance agent

The ideal place for safekeeping important papers such as deeds, mortgages, bonds, stock certificates, birth certificates, marriage or cohabitation agreements, inability mandates, citizenship papers and diplomas and educational certificates, as well as lists and photos of articles protected by theft or fire insurance, are deposit boxes.

When documents are placed in a plastic envelope, they are protected from humidity, and if you keep them at home, be sure that they are kept all together in an organized manner and stored in a safety deposit box, which can be bought from office supply stores.

When a death occurs in the family, it is good to know who to contact in order to obtain information about the benefits to which the family, beneficiaries and other people are entitled.

- If the deceased was employed, the family should contact the employer to find out what benefits are payable (group life insurance, pension fund, unpaid commissions, etc.).

- If the deceased was retired, the family should contact the organization that was paying the pension.

- If the deceased was a veteran, the family should contact the nearest Veterans Affairs Canada office, as they may be entitled to benefits.

- If the deceased worked for the federal or provincial government, the family is entitled to benefits.

- If the deceased was a member of a union, professional association or club, the family may also be entitled to benefits.

Various forms are available at Canada Pension Plan and Regie des Rentes du Quebec offices, including applications for survivor, orphan and death benefits. When applying for death benefits, the birth and death certificate and the social insurance number of the deceased are required. To obtain survivor's benefits, the spouse must provide both a birth and marriage certificate. If you are a common-law spouse, you may be eligible for survivor's benefits if you lived with the deceased for at least three years prior to his or her death. If a child was born or will be born as a result of your union, or if you adopted a child together, only one year of cohabitation is required. Finally, you must present a birth certificate for each child who is entitled to benefits. Other documents may also be necessary depending on the circumstances. Your financial advisor will provide your family with all the necessary information on your insurance portfolio and assist them in filing out the forms required to file claims.

In addition to the policy, life insurance companies generally require at least two documents to establish the validity of a claim: the policy beneficiary statement and a death certificate or a statement by the attending physician. In some cases, other documents may also be requested. If the beneficiary is a minor, is legally incompetent or is also the estate, other formalities will also apply.

Your advisor can also help your family choose the most appropriate form of settlement for the death benefit. For example, it can be paid in a lump sum, paid in instalments or deposited in an account and left to earn interest. Your financial advisor is well versed in the advantages of each option and will explain each one clearly.

Finally, it's important to carefully read the deceased's insurance policies as they pertain to disability coverage, hospitalization expenses, surgical fees and more.

There are a number of matters that the estate executor or members of the family will have to look after. Certain debts (such as mortgage loans, service contracts and credit card balances) will have to be settled. This is easily taken care of if the deceased took out a temporary life insurance policy designed specifically for this purpose. Contact the companies in question to find out if any such arrangements were made.

Since other debts will also have to be paid, you should contact your banking institution as soon as possible in order to request the release of any amounts contained in joint accounts. Legislation varies from province to province, but banks and insurance companies are generally allowed to pay out certain amounts in advance, even if the will has not yet been probated. Finally, if there is a transfer of property, especially a house or car, insurance policies will have to be modified accordingly. Contact your general insurance agent to have this taken care of.

Barriers to some of your goals might include:

a. Insufficient life, critical illness, long-term care or disability income insurance to meet goals and objectives. You need financial tools to replace your income that is lost when you as a wage earner die or become disabled. It is the perfect solution to your loved ones, partners and dependents against financial hardship or loss. If you have sufficient financial tools, you have peace of mind that your family will not be loaded with debt when you are gone, get sick or become disabled. Your mortgage will be paid off, creditors will be paid and some money may be left for your ultimate tax bills.

b. Debt load. Debts are burdens to your family. Do you have sufficient life insurance to pay off your debts?

c. An ineffective strategy. Are you mapping steps to become financially fit?

Things You Should Know

Tax Won't Disappear in Case of Death

When a person dies, there is a "deemed disposition" of all capital property. This means that the government treats all your property (unless jointly held) such as stocks, bonds, RRSPs and real estate as sold at fair market value on the day of your death. Your estate will be required to pay capital gains tax on that property. This applies to your RRSP if you do not have a spouse to whom you can transfer it. Careful planning can reduce or defer the taxes owing. Without an estate plan, you could lose nearly half of the value of your gains to taxes. Though your executor may claim full personal exemptions on your final income tax return, your estate may end up paying taxes at the highest tax rate (more than 50 percent).

You should seek independent tax advice on the following issues.

1. *Capital Beneficiary of a Testamentary Spousal Trust*

A testamentary spousal trust is created on the trustor's will, instructing to provide for the spouse until he or she dies.

For example, a capital beneficiary of a testamentary spousal trust that was established for your mother on your father's death as the trust was being wound up. As a sole beneficiary of the trust, he was entitled to receive all of the trust property and therefore wanted to be advised on the following:

- Taxes owing on the property transferred to you

- The value of the shares being transferred

- The tax consequences if you sold those shares

- Tax implications if you set up a trust with the transferred property for the benefit of your wife or children

This beneficiary would need expert tax advice to determine:

- The cost base of the transferred property

- The cost base of the transferred shares

- The tax implications of using transferred property to set up a trust for your survivors

2. *Determination of "Death Taxes" Owing on an Estate*

On your death, "everything" was transferred in your will to your surviving spouse at their cost base. At the death of your spouse, the surviving children need assistance in calculating the amount of income tax payable before the assets can be transferred to themselves.

- Estate assets are subject to probate fees.

- Each estate asset must be reviewed in order to determine the amount of tax payable.

- Expert advice is needed to determine the taxation issues relating to the disposition of the estate.

3. *A Messed-Up, Self-Directed Registered Retirement Savings Plan (RRSP)*

You should consult a tax expert to get the best advice on the most cost-effective of resolving your tax problems if:

- Your self-directed RRSP has a foreign content well in excess of the 30 percent limit, and is subject to a penalty tax until the foreign content is reduced to the acceptable limit.

- Your RRSP also contains investments that are not qualified for RRSP purposes.

- You have been depositing cash and contributions in kind into his RRSP.

Planning Ahead for Taxes

There's a good chance that taxes will be owing to the federal and provincial government upon death. There may also be capital gains and recapture of depreciation. A final income tax return will therefore have to be filed. In some cases, it may even be advantageous to file a second return, which is called a separate return. Tax returns are usually looked after by the legal advisor or accountant handling the estate.

Insurance Solution for Tax Problems For Individuals and Families
#1 RRSP Benefits for a Single Person

Jason is a divorced father of two children and wants to pass on to his children as much of his RRSP as possible, if he dies soon after retiring. Upon the death of Jason, the RRSP will be considered disposed of, and the entire value will be included as ordinary income in his final tax return. If he wants to pass on the RRSP benefits to his children, the tax owing would reduce the RRSP value by as much as 50 percent.

Jason can apply for life insurance to address the tax problem. If he dies before retiring, with an appropriate amount of life insurance on his life and his estate as beneficiary, his estate will receive the death benefit. The children can use the proceeds to pay the tax owing on the value of the RRSP. All of the funds from the RRSP can then be distributed to the children.

If he lives to receive an annuity from the RRSP, he can select a life-only annuity. The annuity payments would stop upon his death, and there would be no taxes payable. The insurance proceeds paid to his estate could be distributed to his children.

#2 Using an Exempt Life Insurance Contract

Nancy is concerned that her investments are generating taxable income each year, and she wants to know how she can reduce the amount taxable on her investments. She is contributing the maximum amount to RRSP and holds sizeable nonregistered investments that yield returns, such as unrealized capital gains, dividend income and interest.

If her insurance program is not sufficient to cover her financial planning needs, an insurance needs analysis should be done. Since her insurance needs are permanent, a permanent life insurance plan should be recommended—for example, a universal life policy (which will be defined in the next chapter). A universal life policy would enable her to tailor the premiums to pay for the insurance over a relatively short period of time.

At the same time, she could invest her premium payments in her choice of investments that would provide a competitive rate of return. As long as she maintains the accumulating funds in her policy below a certain level to keep it tax-exempt, any investment returns will be tax-free. Life insurance benefit is tax-free. She can choose a premium payment plan aimed at paying up her UL policy as a whole life plan within 25 years, and a general fund interest account for the deposit of her premiums.

#3 Taxation of Estate Assets and Joint-and-Last-to-Die Insurance

Mr. and Mrs. Smith wish to establish a financial and estate plan to make sure that their assets—a principal residence, cottage, rental properties and investments in stocks, bonds and GICs—will be transferred in an orderly fashion to their children.

They may seek to discuss with a financial advisor the tax implications of parents transferring their assets to their children when they die. They could be advised to consult a tax accountant to determine the amount of income tax payable at death. The income tax cannot be avoided, and they could dispose of their assets before they die, but they must still pay income tax on the value of their estate. Life insurance in an amount equal to at least the estimated amount of tax owing at death could be made payable to the estate and earmarked to pay the income tax.

They may be recommended to consider a joint life policy, with proceeds payable upon the second death. Upon the first death, the estate assets can be transferred without tax consequences to the survivor, and only upon the death of the survivor would all of the assets be considered disposed of for their fair market value for income tax purposes.

For more information, contact the federal or provincial tax office nearest you, and talk to a knowledgeable financial advisor.

Taxes and Investment Income

There are three different types of investment income: interest income, dividends and capital gains. When investing outside an RRSP, it is important to understand how each is taxed.

Interest income receives no tax-favoured treatment. It is simply added to your income and taxed at your marginal tax rate.

Dividends are payout of a company's profits to its stockholders. To encourage investment in Canadian companies, the government provides an incentive in the form of dividend tax credit. The credit reduces the tax owing on dividends received from Canadian companies.

If you sell or transfer a security or other capital property for more that it's purchase price, you generate a *capital gain.* Capital gains, like dividends, receive tax-favoured treatment. Only 50 percent of your annual net capital gains are added to your income and taxed.

Alternative Solutions

The Mystery of Protection

The ultimate source of protection is insurance. In simplest meaning, insurance is a compensation or reimbursement of economic loss incurred due to uncertain events like fire, theft, accident, loss resulting from liability (to others) for personal injury or damage to property and financial loss resulting from death, disability or retirement (outliving person's capital) by the insurer, for a fee called the premium.

You might wonder how safe life insurance is in Canada. Federal, provincial and territorial regulators require every life insurance company who is authorized to sell insurance policies in Canada to become a member of Assuris. Assuris is a nonprofit organization that protects Canadian policyholders if their life insurance company should fail. Their role is to protect policyholders by minimizing the loss of benefits and ensuring a quick transfer of their policies to a solvent company, where their protected benefits will continue to be honoured. Every policyholder is deemed to be safe.

However, before purchasing financial products, check to make sure you are dealing with licensed agents and companies by checking the Financial Services Commission of Ontario (FSCO) website, under "Who Is Licensed." FSCO is a regulatory agency of the Ministry of Finance that regulates insurance, pension plans, loan and trust companies, credit unions, mortgage brokering and co-operative corporations in Ontario. If you purchase insurance from insurers that are not licensed in the province, they are not protected under the insurance act and the regulations that govern Ontario's licensed insurance companies.

Embracing Insurance Products
Life Insurance

Life insurance can be permanent or for a term. The benefit will pay out when the insured dies. The proceeds pay funeral costs, existing debts and estate expenses, and it creates an estate.

Disability Insurance

In case of disability, employment income is replaced. This is more beneficial to self-employed individuals and business owners. What do you think would happen if you were suddenly unable to work and had less money coming in, plus additional money going out to cover medical expenses and other bills related to your disability? Where would the money come from to replace your lost income? Your lifestyle you enjoy, your children's college education, your savings for a comfortable retirement—these all depend on your ability to earn a living, and they will continue even in the event of being disabled.

Disability insurance may be added to a life insurance policy to pay the insured a monthly income if you suffer a disability. It may also be purchased as a separate, stand-alone policy.

Waiver of Premium for Payor Benefit

This waiver provides that if the owner and premium payor of a juvenile policy dies or becomes disabled, the premiums will be waived until the juvenile is aged 21. The owner and premium payor must provide satisfactory evidence of insurability. If the disability is due to accident or illness, the premium's falling due will be waived as long as the disability continues. If the owner and premium payor dies, the premiums will continue to be waived. If the owner and premium payor is disabled for three months or longer, the insurer will waive premiums due on or after the beginning of the disability: Some insurers may require six months of disability before premiums are waived.

Accidental Death and Dismemberment (AD&D)

This policy may be added to all life insurance policies. The insurer will pay the benefit for a serious injury as follows:

- The full benefit will be paid for the loss of both arms or the sight in both eyes.

- A partial benefit is paid for loss of one limb or the loss of sight in one eye.

Critical Illness

The critical illness policy will pay a lump sum once the payor is diagnosed with critical illness. It's a good help financially while you are recovering.

Critical illness was introduced in Canada five years ago. This kind of insurance was introduced by Dr. Marius Barnard, the brother of Christian Barnard, the doctor who performed the first successful heart transplant surgery in South Africa in 1983. Marius Barnard saw the need for insurance that paid a living benefit to those who survived major illnesses, to offset lost income and to pay additional expenses.

Illness and the road to recovery can be difficult and draining on an emotional, physical and financial level. If it strikes on you, who will take care of your financial worries? This kind of insurance pays you when you get sick, and you may get the option to refund all the money you paid if you don't get sick. Most or almost all insurance companies offer different types of illness coverage, and all of them cover any kind of cancer (life threatening), stroke and heart attack. A few other covered illnesses are Alzheimer's, bacterial meningitis, coma, coronary artery bypass surgery, loss of independent existence, loss of limbs (dismemberment), motor neuron disease, multiple sclerosis and Parkinson's.

There is also a term and permanent plan on critical illness, and you have the option to put some benefit rider, like waiver of premium upon disability or refund of premiums on the 10th year, 65 years old or 75 years old.

Every company offers different types of critical illness. The three deadly diseases—cancer, heart attack and stroke—are always included.

Terminal Illness Benefit

This benefit pays a portion of the death benefit to the policy owner if the insured suffers from such an illness. It specifies in the contract the amount of benefit, usually a percentage of the policy's face amount up to a certain maximum. When death occurs, the final death benefit is reduced by the amount paid out as a terminal illness benefit, and the beneficiary stated in the contract will receive the difference. A physician must certify that the insured's life expectancy is 12 months or less.

Accident and Sickness Insurance

This insurance covers medical services that are not covered under provincial plans like ambulance services, eye care, hearing aids and semiprivate and private hospital ward accommodation.

Travel Insurance

Travel insurance covers unexpected costs incurred due to medical emergencies. You may customize a plan depending on your need before and during your trip. You may purchase trip interruption, flight accident, accidental death and dismemberment and rental car collision damage protection. It also covers delayed baggage, cancellation by the tour operator, lost and damaged baggage and personal effects and default of travel supplier, but there are exclusions. Be sure to read policy before you travel, to review what you purchased.

Mortgage Insurance

Mortgage insurance is also known as mortgage life insurance or creditor insurance. It is an insurance that repays the mortgage of a debtor or investor in case the person passes away. Purchasing a house is the biggest investment you will ever make, so it is wise to protect your investment. If you arranged your mortgage with a bank, they asked you to purchase the insurance mortgage protection with them, but most banks underwrite your policy once death claims arise. On the other hand, insurance companies underwrite upfront and notify you if you are approved, rated or denied, and once a claim arises, there are no questions asked. Life insurance companies offer you more options and a better control of your mortgage protection. Here are some comparisons.

Insurance Companies	Bank/Lenders
Your beneficiary is your family	Bank/lender the beneficiary
Portable: if you move, your protection stays	If you move, your protection terminates
Premium does not charge interest	Your premium incorporates with your amortization, so you may pay extra
A licensed advisor will assist you	Bank employee will look after you
Coverage stays during the term you have chosen	Coverage is decreasing based on 5-year term

You are insured under an individual life insurance policy	Issued under a group insurance by the insurance company
You own the policy	Bank/lenders own the certificate of insurance
You can change your plan or convert to permanent without evidence of insurability	No guarantee to renew for a new mortgage; must provide new evidence of insurability

Check with your local licensed financial advisor or insurance agent for updates. Insurance companies develop new plans from time to time to meet your needs and to find out about every aspect of your financial security.

Long-Term Care Insurance

This coverage provides benefits to cover expenses of a disabled insured who is unable to perform the activities of daily living (ADL). It pays benefits if the insured cannot perform two or more ADLs such as eating, bathing, dressing or moving without assistance. It pays for a range of services not covered by medical insurance programs, such as:

- Adult day care

- Home health care

- Nursing home care

- Residence in a skilled nursing facility

- Residence in an assisted living facility

- Residence in an Alzheimer's facility

- Caregiver respite care

Coverage is often associated with people at or near retirement age. It is often renewable for the lifetime of the insured, or until the maximum lifetime benefits have been paid out.

As a rider to a life policy, LTC provides a monthly benefit to the policy owner if constant medical care is required. The benefit is usually a percentage of the policy's death benefit (face amount). Eligibility for coverage is defined in terms of the inability to perform the ADLs (retroactively) at a later date and is lost. If the base policy has a waiver of premium benefit, and the insured is disabled on an option date, the insurer will automatically issue the additional insurance coverage. Premiums on the additional coverage will be waived until the insured recovers or dies.

Mortality rate in Canada is getting low. But what is the likelihood of needing long-term care after age 65? Long-term care support reaches 43 percent of seniors.

Should your spouse or parent or you need care, long-term care at either a facility or at home is the way to go. The cost of care and the coverage gaps that exist in provincial health insurance plans and the expenses are costly. Preferred accommodation cost in Ontario for a long-term stay at a government-subsidized nursing home is $2,166 per month. Privately owned retirement residence average cost approximately $1,600–5,000 per month for semiprivate, and private is around $1,600–8,000. Government subsidies are not available for private facility care.

Some expenses for private nursing, cooking, cleaning, shopping and more will be largely your responsibility.

Without proper planning, the cost of long-term care will drain your savings, assets and retirement income.

Extended Health Insurance

This protection is used to supplement provincial health insurance coverage and to cover prescription drugs, dental care, vision care, private duly nursing, private or semiprivate hospital accommodation and paramedical services.

Automobile Insurance

This protection can be used to pay third-party liability costs, accident benefits and damage to a vehicle.

Homeowners' Insurance (including tenant packages)

This protection is used to protect property, to provide liability coverage for owners in case of accidents on private property and to protect the contents of a house or apartment.

Commercial Property Insurance

This protection is use to compensate a business for losses caused by fire or theft.

Liability Insurance

This protection provides errors and omission coverage, and it protects an insurance agent from financial losses once sued.

Annuities

Annuities provides regular income payments, creating an income stream.

Group Insurance

This insurance is offered by employers to benefit employees and may cover their dependents, which include life, disability accident and sickness protection. It's normally issued without medical examination. Benefits end once the employee resigns or retires. An employee has the option to carry over the benefits by talking to a broker that has a contract with the carrier.

All about Life Insurance

Most of us really don't know how much insurance we need. Every individual or family has different cases or situations, and therefore different financial analysis. You could do a simple analysis, but a trained and licensed life insurance agent can help you.

Here are some expenses to deal with once death occurs.

- Permanent: Funeral expenses, estate taxes, medical expenses and income replacement

- Temporary: Mortgages or rental, day care costs, tuition fees and loans or credit cards

Once you know what you own and what you owe and what expenses are to be incurred, you will know about how much life insurance you need to replace your income and cover expenses in case of death. A simple analysis to replace one's income is seven times your net income.

The amount of insurance needed depends on three variables.

Cash Needs

Determine how much you will need to meet immediate obligations such as funeral, medical and legal expenses and paying off debt and tax liabilities.

Income Needs

Apply the rule of thumb: multiply seven times your annual income. How much is your future income required to sustain your surviving family members? Alternatively, use the following calculation.

Using Human Life Approach

Basic calculation:

Economic value of human life = <u>Amount of income required</u>
Prevailing interest rate

Example

Jason, 35 years old, is the breadwinner of the family and earns $35,000 per annum. The prevailing interest rate is 5%.

<u>$35,000</u>   or   <u>$35,000</u>

  5%   .05

The insurance amount required to replace the economic value is $700,000.

Basic calculation including inflation:

Economic value of human life = <u>Amount of income required</u>
Real rate of Interest

Example

The Smith family earns $60,000 per year and currently

has a term coverage of $250,000. If the nominal interest rate is 5% and a long-term inflation rate of 2%, then:

Real rate of interest = 5% - 2% = 3%

$$\frac{\$60,000}{3\%} \quad or \quad \frac{\$60,000}{.03}$$

Amount of insurance required is $2,000,000.

Minus current coverage ($250,000)

Additional insurance amount needed =$1,750,000

Using Capital Needs or Capital Retention Approach
Assets Availability

Know your inventory. You should know how much you have to cover the immediate cost needs and future income needs.

The basic calculations are as follows.

Example

The Smith family needs to protect against the death of Jason, who is the principal income earner.

Scenario:

Insurance coverage on main breadwinner is $30,000

Total family assets $250,000

Final expenses $300,000

Continuing annual income sources $25,000

Continuing annual income needs $40,000

Expected rate of return 5%

1. Cash needs = assets - final expenses

$250,000 - $300,000
= $50,000 shortfall
2. Continuing income needs = continuing income sources - continuing cash needs

$25,000 - $40,000
= $15,000 shortfall
3. Capitalized value of continuing income needs =

$$\frac{\text{Continuing income needs}}{\text{prevailing interest rate}}$$

Capitalized value of continuing income needs =

$$\frac{\$15,000}{5\%}$$

= $300,000
4. Insurance required = capitalized value of insured's life + cash needs

Continuing income needs = $300,000
Add shortfall of cash needs $50,000
Amount of insurance needed = $350,000

Kinds of Insurance
In general there are two kinds of life insurance in Canada: permanent and term insurance. Permanent could be categorized as whole life and universal life, and term insurance is designed for temporary financial needs.

Whole Life
Whole life has these distinguishing features.

1. It has a cash value: It accumulates savings in a certain year; normally starts after four years.

2. Cash value will be given to the insured if he chose to surrender his policy.

3. You may choose to use the cash value to pay some of the coverage.

4. You may take a loan from the cash value up to 90 percent. This loan is an interest-bearing loan.

5. Premium stays the same.

Remember that you are paying for the coverage that your named beneficiary will receive in case of death. Cash value is an added feature only, and you can take advantage of it while you are alive.

Whole life has these different plans.

1. Whole life paid up in 10 years. You only pay the premium in 10 years, and you are protected the whole of your life.

2. Whole life paid up in 20 years. You pay the premium in 20 years, and you are protected lifelong.

3. Whole life paid up in 65 years. You pay the premium until you reach 65, and you are covered till the end of your life.

4. Regular whole life. You pay the premium as long as you live without increasing the premium, and you may choose to pay it up by using its cash value at a reduced coverage in a certain time.

Universal Whole Life
This type of insurance is the answer for the advice of "buy term and invest the difference." This permanent

life insurance has an investment option to choose from, similar to mutual funds. Mortality charges are disclosed and administration charges are identified. Cost of insurance and administrative cost and investment portion is shown in the illustration. Cost of insurance can be level (never goes up) or annual renewable term (cost will increase annually).

You should know the advantages of this type of insurance. Universal life insurance provides two financial planning solutions: a savings component that permits tax-deferred investment growth and life insurance that provides a tax-free death benefit (which includes your savings and your insured amount). When you deposit premiums into a UL plan, part of your money goes toward savings, and part of it pays for your insurance protection and administration fees. The growth of funds inside the policy is tax-free; you do not pay income tax on the growth. Creditors cannot get the funds in said policy; they are creditor-proof if the policy is set up properly. In the case of the insured's death, the entire investment account, the face value of the insurance policy, goes to the named beneficiary or beneficiaries, tax-free. In case of disability, you also withdraw the funds without paying tax, and you can invest 100 percent of the savings and investment component in an index where the returns are based on the performance of an index outside Canada.

Some insurance companies offer options to pay off the premiums in 10, 15 or 20 years, and you are covered or protected for a lifelong guarantee. A broker or an associate agency who partners with different insurance companies can tell who offers the limited pay option plan.

Term Insurance

Term insurance is the best type of protection for your temporary needs. As I mentioned earlier, that includes mortgages, loans, credit cards, day care and educational fees. There are different terms from which you can choose.

- Term 10: You are covered only for 10 years, and you may renew it for a higher price.

- Term 20: Your protection runs longer, but at the end of the 20th year, the premium will be drastically higher.

- Term 75: This expires at the age of 75.

- Term 100: You are protected as long as you pay the premium, till death. Once you reach the age of 100, depending on the policy provision, the coverage will be awarded. The premium stays the same throughout.

You may also pick a term at whatever period of protection you want (i.e., 7 years, 15 years or 30 years). This is great for short-term loans and mortgages. Not all insurance companies offer this option. Most companies allow you to convert your policy to permanent insurance without evidence of insurability before you reach the age of 65.

You may also want a mix plan, like term insurance riders on a permanent life insurance policy. The purpose of this is a convenient way of arranging an individual's and a family's insurance plans. The term rider may cost less than a separate term policy providing the same coverage, because the policy fee is smaller or is waived for the term rider. The term rider will continue in force under the automatic premium-loan, nonforfeiture option of a permanent policy that has sufficient loan value. The term riders allow policy owners to address a range of insurance needs that require permanent insurance or temporary insurance, or a combination of both in one policy. The term coverage can be either terminated or converted to permanent insurance as circumstances change.

Term Coverage for a Spouse or Children

An insurance program may cover the spouse and children in a family fewer than one policy. Term coverage for a spouse may be arranged to provide care for minor children if the spouse insured under the term dies. Term coverage on children can cover the funeral costs and other costs associated with the death of a child. Coverage is usually based on units of coverage.

Do It Now

It is a precise decision. This time is the right time, not tomorrow, because tomorrow may be when you need it. Why not act now?

The cost of insurance is based on age and gender. The most common insurance calculations are those involving age and gender, and those used to determine the premium to be charged for a particular policy. For example, if you are a smoker, your rate will be higher.

Age
Some insurers quote premiums based on the "actual" or "current," and others on your nearest birthday.

If age is based on the current age attained, a client born May 6, 1975, who applied on February 28, 2011, would be considered 35 years old:

Year of last birthday	2010
Year of birth	1975
Age in policy	35

If age is based on the nearest birthday, he would be considered 36.

Date of application	2011
Year of birth	1975
Age in policy	36

Smoking Status

Most insurers offer preferred premium rates to nonsmokers. Some insurers describe nonsmokers' premium rates as standard rates, and the rate for smokers as substandard rates. Applicants who have not smoked a cigarette or used tobacco products within the last 12 months are eligible for nonsmoker rates.

Within the first two years of a policy, the insurer can cancel the contract upon discovering that the applicant made material misrepresentations on the application. Failure to disclose a smoking habit is considered a material misrepresentation. If the policy has been in force more than two years, the insurer must prove that the applicant acted with fraudulent intent to make the insurer issue the policy on a nonsmoker basis.

Modifying the contract to reflect the fact that the applicant is a smoker may not be upheld in the law-governing insurance contracts.

Provincial legislation governing insurance contracts allow insurers to modify a contact for two reasons only: If the age or the sex of the applicant has been misrepresented.

How much does insurance cost the Smith family assuming both spouse are 35 years of age, are nonsmokers and are in good health?

If Jason is the principal earner, and if he dies today, the capital retention amount needed by the family is $350,000.

	Without benefit cost per month	With waiver of premium of disability cost per month
Term 10	$22.59	$24.04
Term 20	$33.62	$36.17
Term 30	$55.62	$60.28

Joint first to die on the life of Mr. and Mrs. Smith for $700,000.

Monthly cost:

    Term 10 $50.22
    Term 20 $85.77

Joint first to die on the life of Mr. and Mrs. Smith for $1,750,000.

Monthly cost:

    Term 10 $113.18
    Term 20 $203.65

Joint last to die on the life of Mr. and Mrs. Smith for

$1,750,000. Last-to-die coverage is a good protection for estate preservation.

Term 10 $69.53
Term 20 $102.60

Smith Family Scenario Sample

The couple bought a townhouse worth $375,000, and the mortgage balance is $325,000. They plan to pay this off in 20 years. They have Kriz, age 16, and Jake, age 15. For 10 years they need at least tuition allowance and cost of living allowance of $500,000. The spouses are thinking of a last expense allowance for $50,000 each.

A mix plan may be purchased. Assuming both are 35 years of age, are in good health and are nonsmokers:

Whole life coverage (permanent expense) $50,000

Term 10 coverage (tuition, daily expenses) $500,000

Term 20 coverage (mortgage) $325,000

Total coverage needed $875,000

Total cost per month:

Mr. Smith = $88.94

Mrs. Smith = $69.87

Both spouses = $158.81

(The above-mentioned costs are based on November 2012 illustration software. The insurance company may change rates with advance notice to financial advisors.)

Perform Periodic Reviews and Updates

a.   Things change and needs change

One transition to another can occur: going from single to married, kids growing up, becoming single again. If any of this applies to you, an update on all documents and plans you have is necessary.

b.   Ensure your plan remains practical and effective

Talk to your financial advisor for any questions you have. You may also search the Internet to find answers to your questions.

Every year you might generate and keep too many papers, so it's a good idea to sort through them from time to time and dispose of those that are not really necessary. But be careful—what may seem irrelevant to you might be very useful to your heirs.

CONCLUSION

I just let you ride on the Behemoth, a metaphor for cancer's journey—the ride that everyone wishes not to experience. What could be the possible solutions to reduce and avoid recurrence of such a disease? What are the things to do and change when an unforeseen event happens? Are you emotionally and financially prepared if you or your loved ones face cancer? What if you are crippled or die due to an illness tomorrow?

It was painful and difficult to accept when my doctor told me that I had cancer. I was in denial for a while and did not want to mingle with people, especially when the mastectomy was done and when the chemotherapy treatment began. I couldn't do anything for a while, and I felt that I was a burden to my family.

Modern reconstruction using microsurgery is an amazing procedure that makes you whole and beautiful again, and I am glad that I did it and got back my self-confidence.

Good lifestyle and healthy eating habits prevent diseases. I researched foods that helped avoid recurrence, as well as activities to do, and I wanted to share them with everyone. Any kind of support—spiritually, financially and emotionally—from friends and family and even neighbours will give hope and strength. I truly appreciate the passion and care of my health-care team and hospital staff; I felt loved and saw God in them, and that made me accept my reality.

The phrase "many lose their health to make money and then lose their money to restore their health" is so true if you do not plan ahead. If on day one of your job, you did not pay for yourself first, then there is nothing for you tomorrow. One should be prepared for the following unforeseen events in our lives—disability, critical illness and death. I suggest the HUG KISS method, which stands for "How U Get to Know Important, Simple Steps," and which you can do to plan and prepare so that you can continue your normal life in case of disability or illness. When death comes, you can leave a legacy to your family or even friends.

Even after all the treatment has been done, you do well by eating healthy foods, you exercise to get fit and you follow every advice from your health care team, a recurrence of breast cancer might still happen. Do not blame yourself.

We don't know where and when our life takes us, so attend that high school reunion to reunite with your old friends to rekindle that young feeling, and spend quality time with your family. I am contemplating and focussing on getting better: I would like to see the future of my kids and perhaps see my future grandchildren.

ABOUT THE BOOK

Cancer is a behemoth that strikes one's life, a ride that is far from over and that alters the way you live. There are ways to fight, stay strong and be healthy. Love and sincere support from family and friends can give you hope and strength, and the HUG KISS method has to do with financial health and protection for life.

This book is an additional resource for people who are suffering from breast cancer, or who know someone who suffers.

ABOUT THE AUTHOR

Arl T. Cornell has been a financial advisor for 17 years, and she is a dedicated person who already serves hundreds of individuals and families with loss and sickness. She has been a mortgage broker for five years. She truly felt how it was to be stricken by an illness and was inspired to write this book to share her experience and knowledge. For any queries and advice, you may contact her at arlTcornell@ridingthebehemoth. com.

**If I am well today, it is thanks
to my health-care team.**

Dr. Nadine Norman
General Surgery, RCPSC
Specialist
Graduated at the University of
British Columbia

Dr. Henry Krieger Medical
Oncologist at the Scarborough
Hospital since 1975

Dr. Danny Vesprini BSc, Molecular Biology and Biotechnology, McMaster University; MSc, Immunology, University of Toronto; MD, University of Toronto; FRCPC, Radiation Oncology

Dr. Sarah Wong MD, FRCS(C) MD, University of Calgary Plastic Surgery Program, McMaster University; board-certified plastic surgeon with the Royal College of Physicians and Surgeons of Canada, specializing in aesthetic and reconstructive breast surgery and body contouring

Family Doctors

Dr. Judith Nacua Bacalso

Dr. Erum Haider

BIBLIOGRAPHY

"A Guide for Women Living with Breast Cancer," *Breast Cancer and You* (Ontario: Amgen Oncology, Amgen Canada Inc., 2006).

"Understanding Treatment for Breast Cancer: A Guide for Women," Canadian Cancer Society, 2006.

"Breast Cancer: Understanding Your Diagnosis," Canadian Cancer Society, 2007.

"Eating Well When You Have Cancer: A Guide to Good Nutrition," Canadian Cancer Society, 2008.

The Community Diabetes Education Program of Ottawa, 2009.

William Newman, "My Plate," *New York Times*, June 2, 2011.

"What Makes Your Plate," Sudbury & District Health Unit, accessed November 28, 2012, http://www.sdhu.com.

Leslie Beck, RD, "Foods That Fight Disease" (Ontario: Penguin Group, 2010), 54–57, 68, 77–84, 224.

"Flavonoid as Cancer-Fighting Factor," January, 23, 2013, http://foodproductdesign.com/articles/2007/08flavonoidcancer-fighting-factor.aspx.

"Nutrition for Everyone," accessed August, 22, 2012, http://cdc.gov/nutrition/everyone/index.html.

"Safe Food Handling in the Home, last modified January 12, 2012, http://www.healthycanadians.gc.ca/eatingnutrition/safety-salubrite/safety-grocery-epicerie-salubrite-eng.php.

"Safe Food Handling," accessed on February 29, 2012, http://www.fsis.usda.gov; http://www.ota.com.

Andy Bellatti, MS, RD, "Eating Rules," accessed February 26, 2012, http://www.eatingrules.com/2012/02.

Melissa Ohlson, MS, RD, LD, "The Cooking Oil Comparison," February 26, 2012, http://www.healthclevelandclinic.org.

"Food Safety," accessed February 26, 2013, http://www.eatrightontario.ca/en/articles/food.safety/safefood.

"Canada Food Guide," accessed August 8, 2012, http://www.hc-sc-gc.ca/fn-an/foodguide-aliment/index-eng.php.

"Food and Nutrients: USDA Nutrient Database for Standard Reference Release," accessed August 22, 2012, http://www.ars-usda.gov/nutrientdata.

Matthew Biggs, et al., *Illustrated Encyclopedia: Vegetables, Herbs and Fruits* (Ontario: Firefly Books, Ltd., 2006), 37, 42, 51, 53, 66, 69, 71, 93, 113, 118, 129, 132, 134–5, 172, 476, 499, 482, 497, 499, 506, 507.

Jed W. Fahey, SCD, "Moringa Oleifera," *Trees for Life Journal*, December 1, 2005, http://www.TFLjournal.org/article.php/20051201124931586. Malunggay Maluggay in the Philipines, Sapina in India, Moringa in English, http://www.agribusinessweek.com, http://www.en.wikipedia.ork/wiki/Moringa_oleifera.

"Buying Guide for Vegetables," accessed February 29, 2012, http://www.whatscookingamerica.net/vegetables/vegetablebuyingguide.htm.

Recipes, accessed March 21, 2012, http://www.tofurecipesonsoyfood.com; http://www.barleyfoods.org.

"Life after Cancer Treatment," accessed February 24, 2012, http://www.cancer.gov/cancertopics/ life-after-treatment; http://www.cancer.org, www. MNCancerResources.org.

Richard Beliveau, MD, "Eat to Avoid Cancer," *Toronto Star*, May 3, 2010.

"Top Healthy Fruits," *Canadian Living*, accessed March 23, 2012, http://www.canadianliving.com/health/nutrition/.

Local Fruits, accessed 2012, http://www.getlocal.bc.org.

"Carbs That Burn Fat," Thayes Fitness, accessed March 7, 2012, http://www.thayesfitness.com/ carbs_that_burn_fat_php.

"High Quality Proven Health Benefits," accessed June 7, 2012, http://www.nutraingredients.com.

Wendy Chen, MD, "Soy Intake Is Safe," accessed January 22, 2012, http://www. http://www.dana-farber.org/ newsroom/videos.aspx?spage=1tag=BreastCancer& ssort=0&vid=23072&sdorder=1; MH Ravindranath, et al., "Soybean, Anti-Cancer," *Exp Med*, 2004, accessed January 22, 2013, http://www.ncbi.nih.gov/ pubmed/15584372; http://aicr.org/press/press-releases/ soy-safe-breastcancer-survivors.html.

"Protecting and Promoting Your Health," accessed June 7, 2012, http://www.fda.gov.

Higgins, et al., "Nutrition and Metabolism," Biomed Central Ltd. (October 6, 2004): doi:10.1186, accessed June 7, 2012, http://www.nutritionandmetabolism.com.

Jonathan Benson, "Discover the Cancer-Fighting Power of Raspberries," *Natural News*, February 11, 2011, http:// www.naturalnews.com/025295_cancer_raspberries_ black.html.

Jonathan Benson, "Carrots and Cruciferous Vegetables Prevent Breast Cancer," *Natural News*, October 23, 2010, http://naturalnews.com/030143_cruciferous_ vegetables_breast_cancer.html.

Rui Hai Liu, "Processed Sweet Corn Has Higher Antioxidant Activity," *Journal of Agriculture and Food Chemistry*, August 14, 2002.

Barbara Turnbull, "When Food Makes You Feel Bad," *Toronto Star*, January 31, 2012.

"Food That Fights Cancer," American Institute for Cancer Research, accessed June 7, 2012, http://www. preventcancer.aicr.org/foods-that-fightcancer/.

Maggie Jones, "How Little Sleep You Get Away With," *New York Times*, April 17, 2011.

"Sleep Deprivation Study," HuffPost Healthy Living Canada, accessed January 19, 2013, http://www.huffingtonpost. com/2011/4/21/sleep-deprivation_n_852037.html.

MH Bonnet, *Sleep Deprivation: Principles and Practice of Sleep Medicine*, 2nd ed. (Philadelphia: Saunders, 1994), 50–68.

Elizabeth Scott, MS, *Stress Management Newsletter*, accessed September 16, 2012.

Advocacy Center for the Elderly (ACE) & Community Legal Education Ontario/Education: Wills, Power of Attorney, March 2008.

Financial Advisors' Pocket Reference, no. B641 (2010–11), CCH Canadian Limited, 1–44. TFSA, News 1130, Ottawa, Ontario, September 1, 2012.

Visit these websites for more information:

http://www.attorneygeneral.jus.gov.on.ca

http://www.clhia.ca

http://www.pwgsc.gc.ca

http://www.serviceontario.ca

www.cra-arc.gc.ca/menu-eng.html

Assumption Life	www.assumption.ca
Bank of Montreal	www.bmo.com
Canada Life	www.canadalife.com
Coruz Insurance Inc.	www.coruzinsurance.com
Desjardins Life Insurance	www.desjardinslifeinsurance.com
Empire Life	www.empirelife.ca
Equitable Life	www.equitablelife.ca
Foresters	www.foresters.ca
Industrial Alliance	www.inalco.com
IDC Worldsource Insurance Network	www.idcwin.ca
Manulife	www.manulife.ca
Royal Bank Insurance	www.rbc.com
Reliable Life	www.reliableinsurance.com
SSQ Financial Group	www.ssq.ca
Sunlife of Canada	www.sunlife.ca
TIC	www.travelinsurance.ca
Transamerica	www.transamerica.ca
UL Mutual	UL Mutual.ca

About Mortgages:

Argentum Mortgages	www. Artentummortgages.ca
Avanti Financial	www.avanti-financial.com

INDEX

Vesprini, Dr. Danny, 151
Vitamins, 76–77
  A, 44, 45, 60, 64
  C, 41, 42, 44, 45, 47,
     60, 63, 64
  E, 41, 61
  K, 61

W
Wigs, 21–22
Wills, 89–92
  versus living will, 104–5
  probate of, 93
Wong, Dr. Sarah, 151

Z
Zinc, 41

www.ingramcontent.com/pod-product-compliance
Lightning Source LLC
Chambersburg PA
CBHW020419290526
45785CB00002B/633